From Memory to History

From Memory
to History

*Using Oral Sources
in Local Historical Research*

Barbara Allen

and

William Lynwood Montell

The American Association for State and Local History

Nashville, Tennessee

Publication of this book was made possible in part by funds from the sale of the Bicentennial State Histories, which were supported by the National Endowment for the Humanities.

Library of Congress Cataloguing-in-Publication Data

Allen, Barbara, 1946–
  From memory to history.

  Bibliography: p.
  Includes index.
  1. Oral history.   2. United States—History, Local—Sources.   3. Local history—Sources.   I. Montell, William Lynwood, 1931–   .   II. Title.
D16.A38   907'.2   81–3485
ISBN 0–910050–51–1   AACR2

Contents

Preface   vii

1 Toward a Fuller Historical Record   3

2 Characteristics and Settings of
      Orally Communicated History   25

3 Identifying and Using
      Orally Communicated History   47

4 Testing Oral Sources for Historical Validity   67

5 Submerged Forms of Historical Truth   89

6 Producing a Manuscript from Oral Sources   101

   Appendix A: The Legend of Calvin Logsdon   115

   Appendix B: Migratory Legends and Anecdotes 157

   Bibliography of Works Cited   161

   Index   171

Preface

> How little of human life is put upon actual record, or even told from our fathers in traditional story! The genealogists, if we are confined thus, are the true historians of the world. They say we are born and die, marry and have children, inherit lands or titles, and transmit them to our posterity. But the tree of life hath a richer foliage than can be traced through the bald branches of a pedigree.[1]

There is an ever-increasing interest in recording local history from the lips of community residents by using oral history methodology. Part of this interest derives from the public enthusiasm generated by *Roots*, the television program based on Alex Haley's book, which derived in part from oral sources, and by other popular publications such as the *Foxfire* books and Studs Terkel's works. A more deep-seated reason for this interest, however, seems to be a growing appreciation for history at the local level, whether

1. Andrew Picken, *Traditionary Stories of Old Families, and Legendary Illustrations of Family History*, 2 vols. (London: Long and Long, 1833), I: v–vi.

it be focused on regional, community, or ethnic groups. With that appreciation has come the realization that the formal sources for documenting local history are often incomplete and inadequate and that much information about the past can be salvaged only by tapping the memories of those who lived through it or remember hearing older members of the family or community talk about it.

Popular interest in oral history coincides with a growing academic acceptance and use of this method of gathering historical information, witnessed by such publications as William Lynwood Montell's *The Saga of Coe Ridge,* Gladys-Marie Fry's *Night Riders in Black Folk History,* and the excellent works of George E. Evans in England. Many colleges and universities have established permanent oral history programs, most of them devoted to projects involving historical research on the national or state level, or on broad subjects such as regional industrial development. The preponderance of *local* oral history projects is sponsored by city, county, and regional libraries and local historical societies, or is undertaken by individuals. While the time and energy devoted to these projects is commendable, the published results are often uneven, and the quality of the publications stemming from them is correspondingly marred by omissions, inconsistencies, and factual errors. Perhaps the major stumbling block for people wishing to use orally communicated information about the past in local historical research is that they are unsure of what oral information is important historically and ought to be recorded. In addition to being unsure about questions of the accuracy of orally communicated history, gatherers of such history may often be at a loss as to how to interpret these materials.

One source of confusion over using oral historical materials lies in the varied nature of the materials themselves. In addition to standard historical information contained in them, these materials include traditional historical narratives inherited from earlier generations; personal reminiscences; family stories; proverbs; anecdotes about local residents and events; local ballads; and legends of local heroes, geographical landmarks, and the like. This disparate array of oral forms and content often confuses local historians attempting to sift the materials for historical information. Some researchers may not know, for example, how to apply standard historical gauges of accuracy to materials that derive from human memory. They may not be able to recognize migratory narratives that are told in the same form for truth in numerous communities around the country. Or, in their quest for factual authenticity, local historians may overlook the potential of factually unreliable traditions to express values, beliefs, and attitudes toward the past—intangibles that influence people's perceptions of the present and are therefore as important as actual events in interpreting local history.

A number of manuals have been published describing methods of setting up oral history programs, conducting interviews, and processing the recorded material. No guidebook exists, however, that sets forth ways to evaluate and use oral materials once they have been gathered. *From Memory to History* is intended to fill that void by serving as a handbook for researchers wishing to tap the rich storehouse of personal memories and community traditions in reconstructing and writing local history. The book is designed as both a descriptive guide to the oral materials available to local historians and as a manual for evaluating and interpreting those materials.

Chapter 1 addresses some general considerations underlying the use of oral sources for local history. These include the relevance and scope of local history, the role of the interviewer within the community, the contributions that oral sources can make to local history, and the differences between folklore and oral history.

Chapter 2 discusses in detail some characteristics of orally communicated history that set it apart from formal, written history, including such traits as disregard for standard chronology, use of visual imagery in storytelling, and the telescoping of events in time. The second part of chapter 2 describes the settings in which oral information about the past is communicated, including informal conversations as well as formal interviews.

Chapter 3 identifies a number of topics that the local historian is likely to encounter in quest of oral information about the past. These include personal and family experiences, occupations, and events and persons in the community's past. Consideration is given to specific ways in which these materials can be used in local history—to fill in gaps and flesh out the written historical record, to document the "everyday" and human sides of history, and to provide primary information about heretofore undocumented areas of a community's past.

In chapter 4, both internal and external tests for validity are presented, against which orally communicated history can be measured for historical content and accuracy. Internal tests include identifying folkloric elements; collating divergent accounts; allowing for embellishment, personal and group bias, and the personality of informants; and evaluating the logic of oral accounts and their conformity with established historical facts. External tests involve corroboration from written sources, physical artifacts, and the historical traditions of other groups.

Chapter 5 is concerned with the ways in which orally communicated history can be evaluated to reveal hidden truths. Such truths can take the form of the open expression of attitudes toward the past, the contradictory views of historical events held by different factions within a community, the embodiment of values and beliefs in otherwise nonfactual accounts, or the focus of oral accounts on key events in the past.

Finally, chapter 6 presents some specific suggestions for incorporating oral historical materials into a written manuscript. The discussion includes information about organizing and editing oral texts, using both summarized and verbatim materials, presenting conflicting points of view in the manuscript, and dealing with technical matters such as footnotes and bibliographic entries.

Much of the material used to illustrate various points was drawn from our own fieldwork in California, Kentucky, Mississippi, Oregon, and Tennessee. Wherever possible and practical, however, we have incorporated examples from other parts of the United States and the world. Since many of our contributors of oral historical information are now deceased, we are extremely thankful that we began tape recording orally communicated history when we did. With the passing of each one of these storehouses of local historical knowledge, we are reminded anew of the prophetic urgency of an African proverb that says, "When an old person dies, a library burns to the ground."

Lynwood Montell
Barbara Allen

Bowling Green, Kentucky
May 1980

From Memory to History

1

Toward a Fuller Historical Record

ORALLY COMMUNICATED HISTORY IS A VALID AND valuable source of historical information, as oral tradition and formal history complement one another. Each body of knowledge possesses qualities that, taken together, form a fuller historical record. Alone, each one is incomplete, but "together they form a harmonious union, with the one offering objective interpretation based upon sound evidence, and the other giving a personalized immediacy, a sense of being there and of participation."[1] By using orally communicated history, local historians can broaden their data base and achieve keener perspectives on the events and forces that shaped local life and thought.

While formal academic historians make a distinction between the university-trained historian who studies local history and the local nonspecialist who is actively interested and involved in local history research and writing,

1. Philip D. Jordan, "History and Folklore," from an address delivered at the Missouri Historical Society, November 4, 1949, quoted by Robert Seager II in "American Folklore and History: Observations on Potential Integration," *Midwest Folklore* 1 (1951): 214.

the term *local historian* will be employed throughout this book to mean a person who researches and writes about local history topics, making no discrimination between formal and informal training in history. We are assuming that the local historian, whether professional or nonprofessional, has acquired adequate training and expertise in historical methodology to pursue research successfully in topics and themes that are often obscure and for which inadequate documentation exists. Both types of local historians are encouraged in the pages of this book to add the oral perspective to historical inquiry. Through a study of orally communicated history, the local historian will be able to understand the relationship of formal history to oral historical traditions by watching the historical record blossom when orally communicated facts are included, and by seeing that the traditions of a people sometimes bear little resemblance to formal history.

The Role of Local History

For centuries, the focus of Western historians has been on documenting the past of large political units; the nation has traditionally been regarded as the smallest meaningful historical unit, although, in recent years, histories of regions and communities have received an increasing amount of attention. From the viewpoint of many academic historians, however, local history written by members of their own ranks is at best an exercise in methodology and otherwise a product of provincial thought, while local history written by amateurs is regarded as nonscholarly in the main and therefore is generally ignored by academic historians.

4

The attitude of scorn toward historians who have demonstrated an interest in the history of local communities, whether such communities be minority or mainstream, was clearly, if somewhat crudely, expressed in the remark of a distinguished historian serving on a panel to review a plea for attention to ethnic and other tradition-oriented community groups: "Who cares about a few obscure Indians?"[2] The implication of that remark is that the history of any small group or community—local history, broadly defined—is insignificant.

In spite of that prevailing attitude in the past, within recent years increasing numbers of historians have shifted their attention from political to social history, and from the national or international arena to the local scene. David Russo's book, *Families and Communities: A New View of American History*, illustrates that shift. Russo contends that people live simultaneously in a hierarchy of communities ranging from the local neighborhood to the nation. Until the end of the last century, he argues, America's living patterns were largely organized on the local level, where the town, not the nation, was the main reference point. Russo views American history as progressive nationalization of life and life styles originally organized at local levels.[3]

While not speaking directly to the point of the relation-

2. Quoted by Richard M. Dorson in the introduction to his *American Folklore and the Historian* (Chicago: University of Chicago Press, 1971), p. ix.
3. David Russo, *Families and Communities: A New View of American History* (Nashville: American Association for State and Local History, 1974). Russo's thesis has yet to be proven, but his argument is supported by Conal Furay in *The Grass Roots Mind in America* (New York: New Viewpoints, 1977). Furay contends that small towns and local life continue to shape the historical consciousness of Americans.

ship of local history to national history, Russo's work supports the notion that local history serves as a microcosm of a nation's history. Trends in attitudes, thoughts, and economic concerns at the national level may first be discerned and documented at the local level. For example, the introduction into a community of more modern mechanized agricultural implements clearly portends increased agricultural production, which in turn is the signal for Congress to begin preparing legislation for a more effective system of price and production controls. Thus local history research can be vital to an understanding not only of the past of a particular community, whether a rural town or a large city, but also of a region's or a nation's past, "by looking at events, personalities, and environmental changes reflected in smaller units. One community's past—changes in the face of the business district, the community's succession of mayors, patterns of local political activity and voting, the movement of ethnic groups—permits us to understand the broader national past with greater precision and insight."[4]

The Range of Local History

The term *local history* usually refers to the study of whole political entities, such as counties. Local history research can indeed document the history of these units from their founding to the present, and can yield excellent

---

4. A. F. Alvarez and Susan C. Kline, *Self-Discovery through the Humanities, I: Exploring Local History* (Washington, D.C.: The National Council on the Aging, Inc., 1977), p. 71.

results.[5] County histories are meaningful and manageable if the researcher-writer starts out with a firmly grounded purpose and then uses extreme caution and discretion during the process of putting the book together.

To study the world around us requires varied historical research, and the focus of local investigations can be on specific time periods, special topics, ethnic and mainstream group history, neighborhood history and family history, as well as political units such as counties or towns. Thus local historians may investigate a church or synagogue built before the Civil War; a labor strike that tore at community cohesion; an urban neighborhood rich in ethnic heritage and customs; great floods that occurred before the system of flood-control reservoirs was built; changing architectural forms and styles in the business district; recent shifts in local voting patterns; the emerging role of blacks on the city council; the decline of the local family farm; the rise in the incidence of violence and crime during the postwar years; the quality of life during the Great Depression. Local historians can perhaps do more significant work with topics such as those, rather than with subjects whose complexity cannot be dealt with satisfactorily in a limited amount of time and publication space. In a word, local history deals with the people and events we know best. In investigating such topics, orally communicated data can be employed both as a complement to formal records and as a rich source of new information, especially

5. An outstanding example of a county history is Harriet DeCell and JoAnne Prichard's *Yazoo: Its Legends and Legacies* (Yazoo City: Yazoo Delta Press, 1976).

when the information obtained documents subjects about which little written information exists. A superb description of logging operations in the Maine woods, conducted by a group of oral historians at the University of Maine, was based almost exclusively on oral sources. Similarly, sparkling oral descriptions of the community relationships surrounding the Piney Woods School in Mississippi, an institution founded by and for black people, were recorded by oral historians at the Institute for the Study of the History, Life, and Culture of Black People at Jackson State University.

Ethnohistory and Folk History

When the local history topic one chooses to research deals with a subject or a group of people about which very little information exists in written records, the past must be reconstructed almost entirely from oral sources. That reconstruction can be done from two different points of view, and the distinction between them is important.

The first kind of reconstruction pertaining to little-documented groups is called ethnohistory. The ethnohistorical method has been employed since the 1940s, primarily by American cultural anthropologists and archaeologists. Like the formal historian who relies on documentary evidence, the ethnohistorian can, and often does, begin with written sources. Because the human subjects of ethnohistorical investigation are usually nonliterate, these written sources were penned by outsiders, such as missionaries, explorers, and colonial officials. The ethnohistorian must, however, pay attention to culture history, culture change, and the relationships of past cul-

8

ture to the present. That can be done effectively only after firsthand fieldwork has been accomplished by the researcher so as to ensure a thorough knowledge of the culture. The researcher also includes in an ethnohistorical study physical objects, including those recovered through archaeology. Finally, the ethnohistorian relies extensively on orally communicated historical data.[6] Thus, the ethnohistorian laudably combines historical, anthropological, and folkloristic methods of research. That approach has been successfully employed to document the history of American Indians and African peoples.[7] The final product of ethnohistorical research is well-documented history that incorporates the oral traditions of the group being studied, while telling their story from the *point of view of an outsider*.

The second way to reconstruct the past from oral sources is termed *folk history*. In reconstructing folk history, the researcher defines a community's geographical and/or cultural boundaries in accordance with the concepts held by the people who live there, since their statements and feelings about their community may differ sharply from those of outsiders. Since folk history is necessarily oral, it

---

6. Francis A. DeCaro, "Folklore as an 'Historical Science': The Anglo-American Viewpoint" (Ph.D. diss., Indiana University, 1973), pp. 369–374.

7. A splendid example of ethnohistory dealing with the American Indian is afforded in a pamphlet by Richard W. Stoffle and Michael J. Evans, *Kaibab Paiute History, The Early Years* (Fredonia, Arizona: Kaibab Paiute Council, 1978). Published as an article in *Ethnohistory* 23 (1976), under a longer title, this work was purchased by the Kaibab Paiute people and is now distributed by that tribe. Works that focus on African ethnohistory include Jan Vansina's *Oral History: A Study in Historical Methodology* (Chicago: Aldine Publishing Co., 1965), and Daniel F. McCall's *Africa in Time Perspective* (London: Oxford University Press, 1969).

will not be found in archives and libraries, except in unpublished manuscripts that are, themselves, generally based on oral tradition. Thus, obtaining folk history calls for conducting as many tape-recorded interviews as necessary, with carefully chosen informants of varying ages, sexes, and races; obtaining written permission from all informants to use the taped materials; transcribing the tapes' contents word for word; organizing the information gathered in each interview according to chronology or topical categories (the Depression, crime, courtship and marriage, employment practices, life on the assembly line, steamboating); and interpreting what people say in accordance with their own concepts of what is historically significant. The folk historian must also be familiar with published information and archival collections relating to the community or subject under study, using these materials as corroborative evidence when testing oral information for validity.[8]

Both ethnohistory and folk history draw upon the people's own oral recollections, but the two approaches differ in the way the oral materials are presented and interpreted, as Charles Hudson points out:

> The aim of ethnohistory is to reconstruct, using all available materials, what "really happened" in terms that agree with *our* sense of credibility and our sense of relevance. In a folk history we attempt to find what people in another society

---

8. William Lynwood Montell's *The Saga of Coe Ridge: A Study in Oral History* (Knoxville: University of Tennessee Press, 1970) and Gladys-Marie Fry's *Night Riders in Black Folk History* (Knoxville: University of Tennessee Press, 1975) are the best-known folk history studies.

believe "really happened," as judged by *their* sense of credibility and relevance.[9]

The Insider and the Outsider in Local History Research

Most persons who undertake local history research projects are in one sense or another members of the community whose past they are investigating. Being an "insider" by birth or residency can be both an advantage and a disadvantage.

On the positive side, if you are an insider, you will have knowledge of the locations of written records and ways to get at them; you will know the people with whom you will need to consult; you will understand the general background and context of the subject you are investigating; and you will have a general intuitive feeling for the place and the people that comes from long residence in the community. Aside from that specific kind of information, which will facilitate your research efforts, you are a member of the same culture as the people with whom you will be working. You share with them major historical experiences and a cultural system based on similar values, symbols, customs, and attitudes. You will understand nuances of meaning accessible only to someone thoroughly imbued with the cultural values of a specific group. Take, for example, the custom once known to Southerners of giving small children baked sweet potatoes or other tokens of food to pacify them while the adults ate at "the first table." Little Jimmy Dickens's song "Take an Old Cold 'Tater and Wait"

9. Charles Hudson, "Folk History and Ethnohistory," *Ethnohistory* 13 (1966): 54.

had no meaning for a present-day bride from the West Coast until her Southern-born husband explained that it was customary, even during his own childhood, for children to have access to the leftovers only. Misunderstandings can arise from differences, not only between regional cultures, but among different ethnic groups as well. For example, a young Anglo-American woman marrying a Mexican-American man told her prospective parents-in-law that only the "families" of the bride and groom were to attend the wedding. To her, *family* meant parents, sisters, and brothers, while her future relatives understood *family* to include not only immediate members, but aunts, uncles, and cousins as well. She was somewhat disconcerted, therefore, when twenty people more than she had expected showed up for the wedding and the reception. Without the insider's knowledge of the meanings of certain terms, customs, and concepts, a researcher is likely to render a wrong interpretation.

Some of this esoteric, in-group knowledge and perception can, of course, work to one's disadvantage. One may be so close to a subject as to overlook some very obvious aspects of it that an outside reader may wish to know about. Unless such details are recognized and written about, the audience remains in the dark. Some things will be so familiar as to seem not to require explanation, yet an outsider may be baffled by them. A researcher may be hesitant to ask someone about what is known to be a sensitive subject and, conversely, people may be reluctant to talk about such subjects with someone from within the community who knows all persons and factors involved. An outsider in the same situation would not feel the same hesitancy, nor would informants necessarily exhibit the same reticence. The "home-town" researcher's natural emotional involvement with the subject at hand may tend to affect his or her objectivity and lead to an avoidance in exploring unpleasant aspects of it because of personal feelings about it or fear of offending others in the community by bringing it up.

Just as the role of the insider has both positive and negative aspects, being an outsider has both advantages and disadvantages in local history research. The outside researcher can note many facets of a community or a subject that an insider may take for granted. People are more likely to talk freely with an outsider about sensitive subjects, once rapport and trust have been established, than they would with someone they know well. The lack of emotional involvement on the part of the outside researcher is more likely to assure an objective investigation of the subject.

On the other hand, because the outside researcher is unfamiliar with the local scene, he or she may not ask the right questions to elicit information on certain important aspects of a subject. The outsider may bring up an embarrassing subject and yet not know why informants refuse to talk about it. Finally, people may be suspicious of a stranger or an outsider and give false information or even refuse to talk at all. One of our black informants said of his own people, "They can talk to you all day and not tell you anything, if they don't want to."[10] The meaning here is clear: social conversation is cheap and plentiful; talk impregnated with facts comes only after trust is established.

The researcher's sex and ethnic background can also pose

10. Tim Coe, informal conversation, Burkesville, Kentucky, June 2, 1961.

13

methodological problems and can serve as both aid and hindrance to local history research. For example, during a research project investigating the ethnic heritage among Mexican-Americans in Los Angeles, a young woman fieldworker had the following experience:

> While interviewing a young man, the fieldworkers, a man and a woman, raised the subject of childhood games. Drawing upon his own childhood experiences as a means of stimulating the informant, the male interviewer asked the informant to recall games he had played as a child. The female interviewer, it was readily apparent, was unfamiliar with many of these games, and the informant explained in detail for her benefit how the games were played. Had the female interviewer not been present, detailed descriptions would probably have not been provided, for the male interviewer—already familiar with the games mentioned—would not have thought to ask for more than a mere enumeration of games by descriptive titles.[11]

The Contribution of Oral Sources to Local History

Individuals conducting local history research must judge how useful oral sources are going to be for their particular research projects. For topics that are well documented in written form, information gathered orally is useful only tangentially. For other topics, material from memory may often be the only source of information upon which to draw. Most topics fall somewhere between the two; that is, oral sources illuminate the written record, and written history provides the background against which oral histor-

11. Mary MacGregor-Villarreal, "Team Research: Are Two Heads Necessarily Better Than One?" (Paper delivered to the California Folklore Society, Los Angeles, April 1979).

ical traditions may be understood. Oral sources can be used by local historical researchers in three important ways. First, orally communicated history can *supplement* written records; second, it can *complement* what has been documented in formal history; and third, it can provide information about the past that exists in no other form.

Oral Sources as Supplementary Information

Orally communicated history can supplement written historical records by filling in the gaps in formal documents and/or by providing an insider's perspective on momentous events. Interviews with political, military, church, business, civic, and other community leaders are often conducted with these ends in mind. Merrill Miller's biography of President Harry S. Truman and T. Harry Williams's study of Huey P. Long show how information gathered from individuals' memories often provides insights into the decision-making process. Local history researchers might interview the founders and other persons associated with local industries, institutions, and other significant enterprises for the same purposes. Some business concerns, in fact, have employed oral historians to conduct interviews and establish tape archives for the purpose of obtaining and preserving company history. In all instances where the oral record supplements the written, the oral materials remain subsidiary to the written record, although they elucidate certain aspects of that record.

A related use of oral sources as supplement to written records is to provide information about tangible cultural artifacts and objects, such as buildings, equipment and tools, furniture and decorative items, clothing, and the like. One researcher utilized oral sources and on-site fieldwork to reconstruct the architecture (nearly a hundred buildings) from first settlement to abandonment (1881–1960) of the Knott County, Kentucky, community called Head of Hollybush. "Oral history," he wrote, "was an obligatory tool since many of the older log buildings had completely disappeared."[12] He observed in his study that much of the information about these old buildings was passed down as family history. He further commented that "the theoretical framework of much of the study is drawn from buildings existing only in memory. Yet memory proved accurate when it could be checked against legal documents, the only written sources. . . . In addition to the link with family histories, these old buildings remained on the landscape in a reasonably static form over long periods of time, and visual impressions of them permeated the minds of the informants and their parents."[13]

An artifact can be useful in rounding out the historical record only if we know something about its manufacture and function. This kind of information about tools of a trade, for example, can be particularly valuable when such objects are no longer being used and when their original functions may have changed or been forgotten. The same is true for certain architectural features. Take, for example,

12. Charles ("Chip") Martin, Pippa Passes, Kentucky, letter to Lynwood Montell, March 27, 1980.
13. Charles ("Chip") Martin, "Hollybush: The Eclipse of the Traditional Building System in a Mountain Community. An Architectural and Oral Historical Study" (Ph.D. diss., Indiana University, 1980); quoted in his letter of March 27, 1980, to Lynwood Montell.

16

the common pioneer practice in the upper South of extending the roof on a house beyond the house itself at the chimney end. Tradition holds that the projecting roofline sheltered the primitive stick-and-clay chimneys from rain and snow, to prevent the clay from softening and crumbling away from the woody portions of the chimney, which, with the clay gone, would ignite and burn. Later builders of stone and brick chimneys continued to use the extended roof motif, without knowing anything of the original purpose of the protected chimneys.

Two kinds of information about artifactual objects can be elicited from oral sources. First, the process by which the object or structure was constructed and used can be described. That kind of information is especially important and valuable for those who wish to research and document traditional arts, crafts, architecture, and other forms of material culture usually not mentioned in more formal written sources. Second, personal recollections associated with artifacts and structures can personalize those objects and provide a glimpse into life in the past. A local history researcher may record interesting and illuminating recollections of customs associated with the use of artifacts in activities such as churning, washing clothes, and harvesting crops. An informant might recall, for example, that before the days of electric lights the woman of the house regularly sat by the small window next to the fireplace so as to take full advantage of the natural light afforded by the window. That way, she could utilize maximum daylight available, to mend clothes, do other needlework, string beans, and so on. Anyone disposed to help her got a seat at her side.

Oral Sources as Complementary Information

A second use of oral sources is to *complement* the written record by providing an intimate view of the events described. Where formal history tends to be generalized and impersonal, orally communicated history is specific and intensely personalized. Flood, earthquakes, accidents, labor strikes, political contests, and other life-changing experiences are likely to be recounted orally in very personal terms. The following firsthand account of Dust Bowl days of the 1930s in eastern Oregon illustrates this point: "The dust was blowing so hard at times we couldn't even eat at the table. Grandma would throw a sheet over the table so we could eat, the dust was blowing so bad. It was really Dust Bowl days!"[14]

Even accounts offered by descendants of the people to whom these events occurred convey an intimate view of the past. The mass migration to the American West in the nineteenth century, for instance, is described in most formal histories in terms of how many people were involved, what routes they took, and the methods by which they settled the land. The following oral account, on the other hand, shows how the migration was accomplished on the individual level by the narrator's grandfather:

> He took off from Ohio in 1849, I believe. He left, and he got here in 1850. . . . He came with a wagon train, but he had to give the captain of the train so much for the privilege of traveling with him, besides driving an ox team.
>
> So when he landed here, all he had was a rifle and a frying pan and a buffalo robe, besides the clothes he stood in. So that's the way he got west; walked every doggone step from

14. Marge Iverson, tape-recorded interview, Silver Lake, Oregon, July 6, 1978.

St. Joe, Missouri, to Weaverville, up here in Trinity County
[California]. He come the southern route, not across Death
Valley. He just kept coming north; didn't stop to do any
mining. He was looking for land—my grandfather and two
other men were looking for land. It was in the winter-time,
and crossing Mad River they lost their pack mule with all
their food on it, and snow on the ground. . . .

So they kept heading this way, and they come to a place
where they [merchants] had started to carry supplies into the
mines from Humboldt Bay. And it got winter and they built
this lean-to or cache and stored the things that they had
there, which was flour and eggs.

And so one man [with the grandfather] had on an army
overcoat with a lot of padding in the shoulders. So he took
some of that padding out and fired his pistol through there
and got it on fire and got a fire built that way. And they took
their ramrods and made a dough on them by opening a sack
of flour and breaking half a dozen or so of those eggs in
there—he said the eggs weren't very good, either—and
stirred it around with their ramrods until they got a gob of
that dough on their ramrods and then stuck it in the fire. It
made them awful sick but it kept them from starving to
death . . . until they killed some game and then they were all
right.[15]

Oral Sources as Primary Documents

A third use to which oral sources can be put in local
history research is to provide information about a subject
for which there are no or extremely few written accounts.
Kenneth W. Clarke tapped a vein of oral history untouched
by newspapers and local historians, in the northern part of
Warren County, Kentucky, rich enough to enable him to

15. Sid Morrison, tape-recorded interview, Bear River Valley, California, July
26, 1974.

write an account of Uncle Bud Long, his daughter, Janey, and her son, Frankie. The Longs, considered to be on the bottom rung of the social and economic ladder, moved into the Clark's Landing community one night, lived there in stark poverty for a few months, then disappeared, again under cover of darkness. Clarke's reconstruction of their life style, based solely on oral accounts from those who knew the Longs and others who had heard stories about them, is intriguing and valuable, not only for the historical documentation it provides, but also for its insights into community mores, attitudes, and storytelling habits. His analysis of the stories about Uncle Bud reveals much about the delicate process by which oral folk tradition is born, grows, and thrives in the absence of outside influences.[16]

The use of oral sources as original historical information, weighed carefully, is potentially the most valuable and yet, up to now, the least exploited in local history research. Countless untold topics of historical interest could be fruitfully pursued if people's memories were tapped. Without the use of orally communicated material, the task of researching these topics can never be successfully undertaken.

Two cardinal points about the nature of oral tradition need to be restated: first of all, people remember a vast amount of information and a wealth of detail that is never committed to writing; second, what all oral sources have in

16. *Uncle Bud Long: The Birth of a Kentucky Folk Legend* (Lexington: University Press of Kentucky, 1973).

common is the special perspective they provide on the past. Written records speak to the point of *what happened,* while oral sources almost invariably provide insights into *how people felt about what happened.* Written history is, ideally, objective and unbiased, although historians are increasingly coming to recognize the ideal of "objectivity" as illusory, since any historical account is necessarily biased in some respect. Orally communicated history, on the other hand, deriving as it does from the personal experiences of individuals, tends to be more subjective and evaluative, so that individual and community attitudes are clearly expressed in oral accounts of historical events. The following story about a violent encounter between white settlers and local Indians in Humboldt County, California, is especially revealing in that regard. It contains the notion held by the community that Indians should be exterminated and that all whites should take part in the process. In addition to that group attitude, the narrator expresses his own attitude toward such happenings with the question, "So what could he do?":

They had an Indian massacre over on the island in the bay there at Eureka. They massacred a bunch of Indians over there. The Indians were all scattered there—what were still alive—and finally, they run onto this one young Indian—18, 20 years old probably. And he just dropped down on his hands and knees and looked right at them that way. And they told this one man there, said, "You haven't killed any Indians today, you shoot this one." So what could he do? He drew a bead right between the guy's eyes and he touched the trigger, and those old flintlock guns—the flash comes first and then it ignites the powder. And when this young fellow saw that flash, he dropped right down like that, the bullet went over

21

his head and he jumped and ran for the brush and got away from them.[17]

Written Materials Derived from Memory

Although we use the term *oral sources* to refer to information elicited and gathered in conversation, we also use it more broadly to include all materials derived ultimately from memory. While primary materials consist of the spoken word, a good deal of written material is drawn from memory or oral communication and can be used as orally communicated secondary data. The written materials include *letters* (see Appendix A), *autobiographies* (which can include materials derived from oral sources), *family histories, diaries, travel accounts,* and *newspaper columns.* The last source listed is a particularly rich one, for many local-color writers rely extensively on material from oral sources. Herb Caen's daily column in the *San Francisco Chronicle,* for example, is a compendium of current events and historical sidelights intended to illuminate and illustrate life in the City by the Bay. Much of his material is clearly based on orally communicated contributions from readers.

The local historian using printed materials derived from memory needs to bear in mind that written versions are generally more organized, coherent, and concise than oral versions, which tend to be rambling and chronologically disjointed. Furthermore, reminiscences and other interview materials that appear in newspapers and other printed channels may have been edited before being printed. Writ-

17. Sid Morrison, quoted by Barbara Allen in "The Personal Point of View in Orally Communicated History," *Western Folklore* 38 (1979): 115.

ten materials derived from oral sources should therefore take second place to primary information collected in interviews or conversations, where the researcher can ask pertinent questions, to probe more deeply into aspects of the topic that might not have been described in written accounts.

Folklore and Oral History

Up to now, we have intentionally avoided giving types of orally communicated history specific labels, such as *folklore* and *oral history*. Both terms carry meanings and connotations that we wish to avoid. For example, the word *folklore* is sometimes used popularly to designate unverified rumor, falsehood, and hearsay. When people hear or read something that is doubtful, they may remark, "That's just folklore." For our purposes, whether folklore is true or false is immaterial. The fact that it is communicated from one person to another, either orally in face-to-face conversation or visually, by example, rather than being drawn from written materials, is its significant feature for local history research.

The term *oral history* is used in two ways. It can refer to the method by which oral information about the past is collected and recorded, and it can also mean a body of knowledge that exists only in people's memories and will be lost at their deaths. We prefer to think of oral history, therefore, not only as a method of acquiring information but as a body of knowledge about the past that is uniquely different from the information contained in written records. To us, there is little difference between the methods used to collect oral history and those employed in obtaining folklore materials with historical content. Not all oral history is folklore nor is all folklore oral history. Nevertheless, there is a great deal of overlapping between the two fields. Although we deal in later chapters with certain oral forms of expression—traditional narratives, ballads, proverbs—with which folklorists concern themselves, we do not make a distinction between oral history per se and folklore per se. Such distinctions have their usefulness elsewhere, but in a guide such as this, they would serve no real purpose.

2

Characteristics and Settings of Orally Communicated History

ORAL SOURCES USED IN LOCAL HISTORY RESEARCH afford a kind of information about the past different from that contained in written records. Part of that difference lies in the fact that a good deal of what people remember about the past simply never gets recorded. There are other differences between written records and oral sources of information about the past, as well, differences rooted in the very nature of the oral medium by which such information is communicated. Orally communicated history has a distinctive set of characteristics and occurs in a variety of settings.

Characteristics of Orally Communicated History

Most of us are aware that talk about the past differs markedly from what is written about it, but pinning down the exact nature of those differences and their implications for research is sometimes difficult. A consideration of eight characteristics of orally communicated history that seem to have the most definite bearing on local historical research may be helpful. These characteristics include disregard for standard chronology; emotional association of persons as a primary organizing principle; clustering of oral accounts around significant events or persons; reliance on visual imagery and striking detail; compression or telescoping of historical time; displacement of original actors in a historical event with others; migration of dramatic narrative elements among historical accounts; and patterning of oral accounts of different events along similar lines.

Disregard for Standard Chronology

It seems paradoxical for people to talk about *history* without reference to chronology. Yet, in orally communicated history, standard chronology, whether as an over-all framework or as the order of events, is usually missing. The informant who remembers dates accurately is a rare find. More frequently, people place events in time by relating them to other occurrences. Dating events that way may be rather vague, as when an informant says "It happened before the river bottom was cleared"; or it can be precise: "It happened on the day Woodrow Wilson was elected president." Mrs. Ruthie Coe Anders of Indianapolis was able to give the exact year of a murder by recalling her mother's saying that she (the mother) had been permitted to go to a dance on the night the murder occurred, even though she was only eight years old. (The Census Schedule for 1880 indicated that Mrs. Anders's mother was an infant that year, and court records found later verified that the murder had taken place in 1888, when the child was eight years old.) Similarly, Mrs. Rosie Bryant of McCreary County, Kentucky, poignantly associated her family's relocation with the death of her baby:

> We moved to the farm the nineteenth of July in 1927. My little baby had just been dead one month, or lacked one day being dead one month, and I never can forget it. I think of him till today; kills me, nearly.[1]

The relative dating of events by association with other episodes in an individual's life shows how the past becomes most meaningful only when it has been experienced personally. When people cannot speak about events from personal experience, they may simply dismiss such events as having happened "before my time," or they may refuse to discuss them at all, because they feel incompetent to do so.

Epochal events such as the Gold Rush, the Civil War, and the final Indian wars never run together in informants' minds, but people may have no clear idea of the order in which these events occurred or of the lapsed time between them. Persons, places, and events are important in the human perception of history; time is not. As a result, asking questions about the intricacies of chronology may prove frustrating, but that frustration should be instructive, revealing that "for most people the past has not been one of successive waves of disruptive change but one of

---

1. Mrs. Rosie Bryant, tape-recorded interview, Whitley City, Kentucky, May 8, 1979, as part of the Lake Cumberland Library District Oral History Project, Burkesville, Kentucky. The original tape is on deposit at the Kentucky Historical Society Library, Frankfort.

overwhelming continuity."[2] This is not to negate the strength of oral testimonies in recalling details of specific events, but to point out that events are recalled without a chronological frame of reference, perhaps because no causational relationships are recognized among different events.

A second facet of the disregard for chronology in orally communicated history is that the chronological order of events being recounted is usually scrambled. Where formal history is customarily written in narrative form, with events and actions presented in clearly defined chronological progression, *talk* about the past rarely describes events in the order in which they occurred. This does not mean that the order of events in individual incidents is not accurately characterized—otherwise there would be no drama in their telling. It simply means that one incident may be chronologically unrelated to another in the course of conversation. In talking about a local prankster, outlaw, or other character, for instance, incidents from that person's life may be told in a series of stories introduced by such phrases as "one time," "then another time," and so on, although the incident described in the first narrative may actually have happened *after* that recounted in the second. To put it another way, instead of talking in one chronological direction, people focus on a topic and then talk around it. If chronology can be represented as a straight line, the configuration of orally communicated history is best shown as a circle:

2. Quoted by Henry Glassie in "A Folkloristic Thought on the Promise of Oral History," in *Selections from the Fifth and Sixth National Colloquia on Oral History* (New York: Oral History Association, 1972), p. 55.

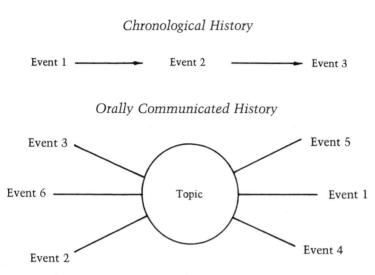

Chronological History

Event 1 ————▶ Event 2 ————▶ Event 3

Orally Communicated History

Event 3

Event 6 ———— Topic ———— Event 1

Event 5

Event 2

Event 4

At the center of the circle is the topic—the exploits of a local strong man, for instance—around which a series of stories is related in random chronological order, so that an event that took place late in the hero's life (Event 5, on a straight chronological time line) might be recounted immediately *before* a story about his initial exhibition of strength (Event 1); other events may be likewise chronologically disarranged in the conversation. Although the lack of a clearly defined time frame or sequence of events may occasionally prove frustrating to the local historian, that lack may be relatively easy to supply by comparing oral information from one person with that gathered from someone else or from written sources.

Emotional Association of Persons as an Organizing Principle

The disregard for chronology in orally communicated

history makes it seem that there is no order at all to the way people talk about the past. Yet there *is* a connecting strand in what is said, although it is quite different from what formal historians might expect it to be. The ordering principle is not time, but the emotional associations that people have with the events and the persons being described. The prominence of these associations is a good indication that the emotional aspect of orally communicated history is perhaps equally as important to the narrators as the historical facts it conveys.

The role of *association* as an ordering principle in orally communicated history is revealed in the fact that oral stories about local historical events are almost invariably embedded, even submerged, in a good deal of talk about the persons involved in the events. That element is brought out in the following bewildering series of connections drawn among the characters in a story being told by Mrs. Mae Wood of Jamestown, Tennessee, about a funeral. "Was that Ott's wife you're talking about?" asked Mrs. Ona Barton.

"No, Ted's," said Mrs. Wood. She turned to her husband and asked, "Did Ott have a wife?"

"Yeah," he replied, "after he got out of the penitentiary, he got him a woman." Once Ott was accounted for, Mrs. Barton turned her attention to his brother Ted.

"They found Ted in the bed, didn't they?" she wanted to know.

"I think so, yeah," replied Mr. Wood.

"But he never did kill anybody, did he?" Mrs. Wood asked, not entirely irrelevantly, since the conversation had up to then dealt with a series of murders in the area.

"I don't know of anybody," said Mr. Wood.

30

"Anyway," continued Mrs. Wood, "I was at the funeral."[3]

At the time, it appeared that Mrs. Barton's questions led the conversation off on an irrelevant tangent, but subsequent encounters with the same kind of meandering discussion have demonstrated convincingly that, for informants, a story is not complete until all the people who play a part in it, no matter how insignificant, have been accounted for, both before and after the event in question.

To someone from outside the community, talk about the local past may seem to wander aimlessly, but to the insider, the progression of the conversation is clear, for it derives from the emotional associations each native has with the people involved in the events being discussed. As a result, the over-all pattern of orally communicated history is not that of a single-threaded discourse. Rather, the relationships among people in the community, which form an associational network, are seen by informants as constituting the human context within which events take place, and those relationships serve as the organizing principle for the order in which events are recounted. Whether listening to people talk about the past among themselves or conducting more formal interviews, the local historian should make note of these patterns of association as a guide to informants' views on the community's past.

Clustering of Oral Accounts

Certain events or persons in the past may, for various

3. Norman Wood, Mae Wood, and Ona Barton, tape-recorded interview, Jamestown, Tennessee, June 18, 1979.

reasons, take on particular significance for a community. When that occurs, a cluster or complex of interrelated narratives develops, each dealing with a different aspect or episode within the larger event of the person's life. The well-known cycles of stories told about historically prominent persons, like Abraham Lincoln and Oliver Cromwell, illustrate this point, as do groups of narratives told about local tragedies, scandals, or other notorious events. Stories surrounding the hanging of Calvin Logsdon in Jamestown, Tennessee, in 1872 afford an excellent example of that characteristic of orally communicated history, for they clustered around three aspects of the event: one group of stories and statements dealt with the murders Logsdon had committed; another described the hanging itself; and a third was concerned with the heavy rain, called the Logsdon Tide, that Logsdon predicted on the gallows and that reputedly followed his execution. (Appendix A presents an analysis of the stories associated with Calvin Logsdon, showing how the local historian can weigh multiple oral accounts in terms of external and internal evidence, to reconstruct a rather accurate, chronologically-oriented, composite account.)

Pointing out that different narratives are told about different aspects of an event does not imply that there is one complete "mega-story" and that individual informants know only fragments of it. Rather, each narrative within a complex is self-contained, though also referring to the larger event with which it is associated. No one person is likely to recall everything about a topic in discussion, since individual narrators respond to and recount those aspects of an event that most appeal to them emotionally. As a result, a significant occurrence in a community's history is likely to stimulate the narrative process in several directions. The resulting narrative complex can reveal a great deal about what people believe to be important events or persons in their community's past. Roughly speaking, the more variety there is in talk about an event or a person in local history, the more significant that occurrence or individual is likely to be in the community's consciousness of the past, and therefore the more deserving it is of the local historian's attention.

Reliance on Visual Imagery

Orally communicated history contains a wealth of images and details that serve to conjure up, in the minds of listeners, vivid mental pictures of the past. The concrete, highly visual terms in which the past is presented in oral sources rivet the listener's attention to the key element of the event described. For instance, the grandson of a Union soldier told the following account of his grandfather's experience of marching with General Sherman:

> He was an old soldier. And he would sit and tell us these old war tales, you know, old war stories. He was in the bunch that marched through Georgia to the sea. And he said when they all got there, to the ocean, he said they was all so hungry that they would eat them oysters without being cooked. He said he felt many a one in his mouth a-kicking while he was eating them. He said he was nearly *starved to death*. He was in the cavalry, in the Kentucky Cavalry.[4]

The point of the story—the desperate hunger of Sherman's

---

4. Sherman Burnett, tape-recorded interview, Wayne County, Kentucky, November 10, 1978.

army—is almost gruesomely made in the description of eating live oysters.

Related to the use of visual imagery in talking about the past is the tendency for people to focus on seemingly trivial details. For instance, stories about the murders committed near Jamestown, Tennessee, by Calvin Logsdon frequently included accounts of the way the victims were discovered, when a visitor saw a lock of a little boy's hair protruding from under the kitchen door. Thinking the little fellow to be lying on the floor asleep, the man reached down and pulled at the hair. He tugged a bit harder when the boy failed to respond. Realizing that something was wrong, the man pushed open the door to find three mutilated bodies. The apparently irrelevant detail of seeing and pulling the child's hair was recounted by more than a dozen informants and was even contained in one of the written depositions sworn during the legal proceedings following the discovery of the bodies.

The picture of the child's hair under the door is not easily forgotten and seems to serve somehow to crystallize the event in the minds of narrators. There is some evidence that traditional storytellers also rely on visual imagery in narrating tales. A Scottish narrator from South Uist, in fact, observed that if he did not visualize the action as he talked, he would be unable to recall the order of events in the story.[5]

Through the use of visual imagery, whole events in a community's history can be compressed into emotionally powerful symbols. In south-central Oregon, for instance, scattered remnants of the homesteading that took place

---

5. Donald McDonald, "A Visual Memory," *Scottish Studies* 22 (1978): 24.

during the early part of the twentieth century are mute reminders of a once-booming past in a now desolate area. An oral description of one such abandoned homestead evokes the sense of futility that the disappointed settlers must have felt when they were forced to leave their homes:

> Well, some of them . . . would go out with a team of horses and they'd haul more stuff than we did. But [two neighboring families], on the morning when they left . . . they drank a cup of coffee there and then they left their coffee cups and plates on the table just as if they were going to go out for a minute and come back. And those cups stayed there for years! There wasn't the vandalism there is now, in those days.[6]

Here the stark image of the deserted house—reported by informant after informant—has become a symbol of the failure of the homesteading effort as a pivotal point in the community's history. In their striking detail and emotional overtones, the verbally painted images of orally communicated history serve to present the past in graphic human terms, expressing a sense of the past as it was actually experienced.

Telescoping Historical Time

In talking about events that actually happened some years or months apart, people frequently omit any mention of intervening occurrences. The result is a telescoped account in which key events or elements in the past are brought into direct association with each other, sometimes to satisfy a sense of the dramatic, sometimes to create a cause-and-effect relationship between the two events thus

---

6. Edwin Eskelin, tape-recorded interview, Fort Rock, Oregon, July 12, 1978.

compressed. This phenomenon has been noted for orally recited traditional genealogies in Africa. Only those generations that have a bearing on the present social and political structure of the society (usually including primeval or mythological ancestors) are included, leaving large blocks of time (by an outsiders' reckoning) unaccounted for.[7]

In our own recording of local accounts of the Logsdon murders, we discovered that many informants claimed the Logsdon Tide came immediately after Calvin Logsdon's hanging, as he had predicted, while others persuasively contended that the two events actually occurred several months apart. Thus, telescoping often reveals to the local historian how people *wish* things had happened, rather than how events actually occurred.

Displacement of Original Actors in Historical Events

In many instances, the central concern in orally communicated history is an action or event; the personalities involved are secondary. When *what* happened is more important than *who* was involved, minor characters may have their identities changed. For example, there are varying accounts of an episode in the career of Beanie Short, a Civil War guerrilla who operated in the Upper Cumberland region that straddles the Kentucky-Tennessee state line. According to one version:

> Beanie had ridden up to the house of John Martin and was threatening him when Martin spoke out and said, "Beanie,

7. Jan Vansina, *Oral Tradition: A Study in Historical Methodology* (Chicago: Aldine Publishing Co., 1965), p. 153.

why are we arguing? We shouldn't have anything against each other." Beanie said, "Well, if you feel that way, I'll leave you alone." Beanie started to ride off, and Martin then shot at Beanie, but killed the horse, instead. The horse fell and pinched Short beneath it. He [Short] then reached his left hand behind his back, around to his gun on his right hip, then shot and killed Martin. It was a clear-cut case of self-defense, but on the tombstone on the Fred Coe place, it reads: "Assassinated by Southern rebels."[8]

Another informant identified Beanie's victim as Sam Biggerstaff, rather than John Martin. The variation in names indicates that the crux of the story is Beanie's marksmanship, and not his target.

That kind of displacement occurs not only with relatively unimportant characters; even the chief actor may be displaced by a better-known or locally more prominent figure. For instance, E. K. Chambers remarked,

> The lapse of folk memory is, indeed, as characteristic as its tenacity. When I passed Athelney last year, a Glastonbury car driver called my attention to the farmhouse in which "Arthur" burnt the cakes. Traditionally, the king who absent-mindedly allowed the peasant woman's cakes to burn was the ninth-century historical Alfred, not the sixth-century legendary Arthur.[9]

Again, comparing oral against written or other oral sources can establish the real identities of actors in historical events. In the example of Beanie Short's vic-

8. D. K. Wilgus and Lynwood Montell, "Beanie Short: A Civil War Chronicle in Legend and Song," in *American Folk Legend: A Symposium* (Berkeley: University of California Press, 1971), p. 140.

9. E. K. Chambers, *Arthur of Britain* (London: Sidgwick and Jackson, 1927), p. 194.

tim, for instance, a tombstone provided the corroborative evidence.

Migration of Dramatic Narrative Elements

Related to the characteristic of displacement in orally communicated history is the tendency for certain striking, exciting, or unusual narrative elements to appear in historical accounts from different time periods or regions, or in association with various personalities. An example of this kind of narrative unit, known as a *motif* to folklorists, is the ineradicable bloodstain, usually associated with the scene of violent or mysterious death, which reappears on walls or floors in spite of repeated washings or recoverings.[10] This particular example is so widespread as to be universal and has been reported from all over the United States, including an account of its appearance on the floor of the Carthage, Illinois, jail, where Joseph Smith, the Mormon leader, was murdered.

Motifs that seem to be limited just to historical accounts (rather than being found in traditional oral fiction) we call *historico-motifs.* Forced overeating, in which food or other substances are poked down an unwilling victim's throat with a pistol barrel or similar object, is one such historico-motif. It has been attributed in various accounts to Beanie Short, who forced an old man to eat a number of puddings; to Jesse James, who supposedly caused a sheriff

10. A six-volume compendium of such motifs (including the ineradicable bloodstain) is *The Motif-Index of Folk Literature,* compiled by Stith Thompson (Bloomington, Ind.: Indiana University Press, 1955–1958). The usefulness of the *Motif-Index* for identifying migratory motifs is discussed in more detail in chapter 4.

to eat a handbill advertising for James's arrest; and to a revolutionary with Pancho Villa, who crammed horse manure down a captive American soldier's throat during the Mexican Revolution.[11] The characteristic feature of these migratory narrative elements is their transferability among stories about different events or persons. While their historicity may sometimes be questionable, they help to provide the visual imagery and embellishmental detail, described earlier as characteristic of orally communicated history, which make a story memorable.

Patterning of Oral Accounts

When people give oral accounts of common kinds of events, such as family migrations to the West, immigrants' encounters with a new culture, or individuals coping with disaster, those accounts tend to fall into patterns in which the same features are emphasized. For instance, a study of the personal narratives told by Jewish immigrants in Toronto showed that informants' stories focused on the hardships of the journey, initial difficulties with language and culture in the New World, and experiences of assimilation.[12] Likewise, traditional family histories tend to focus on pioneer experiences, including the dangers that ancestors faced from weather, wild animals, and Indians, and their resourcefulness in dealing with these threats; how the family fortune was made or lost; or the family's involvement in wars, economic depressions, and other trauma-

11. Wilgus and Montell, "Beanie Short," p. 142.
12. Barbara Kirshenblatt-Gimblett, "Traditional Storytelling in the Toronto Jewish Community: A Study in Performance and Creativity in an Immigrant Culture" (Ph.D. diss., Indiana University, 1972).

inducing occurrences.[13] Finally, oral accounts dealing with outlaws may stress childhood incidents that either foreshadowed or contradicted the individuals' later careers; acts of particular kindness or brutality; and near escapes from the law and from death. By understanding this process of patterning, the local historian can recognize ways in which people remember the past selectively and in conformity with pre-existing models, such as the "good boy gone bad."

In addition to understanding the characteristics of orally communicated history, the local historian needs to recognize the settings in which it occurs and, more specifically, the differences among those settings that produce variations in the way people talk about the past.

Settings Involving Talk About the Past

In using oral sources for local history, the researcher should be aware that obtaining historical information by asking people about it directly is not at all the same as hearing them talk about it in ordinary conversations. There are, in fact, a number of social settings for talking about the past; the formal interview is only one such occasion. The best kind of historical information often comes in conversations in which several people participate, correcting and supplementing each other's oral recollections. Simply stated, different kinds of interactional situations stimulate different varieties of oral historical expression. The following sections describe three basic kinds of settings in which

13. Mody Boatright, "The Family Saga as a Form of Folklore," in *The Family Saga and Other Phases of American Folklore* (Urbana, Ill.: The University of Illinois Press, 1958), pp. 1–19.

people talk about the past, affording the local historian opportunities to collect oral historical information.

Informal Conversations, Informal Settings

Reminiscences about the past of the individual or the community can occur almost any time, in almost any place. Common settings in which people talk about the past on a regular basis include the courthouse environs, where certain older men congregate and chat; the barbershop and beauty parlor, where current news may be interspersed with recollections of past events; the neighborhood store, where customers know each other well and where local news is regularly exchanged; a chance meeting between friends of former years, in which memories are mutually sparked and shared; and family meals, during which spontaneous reminiscing occurs.

Other kinds of conversations besides talk about the past go on in informal settings. People banter, argue, gossip, and exchange news. The historical component may comprise a relatively small proportion of the conversation, over-all, or, as people settle into chairs, it may begin to dominate. A woman in north-central Tennessee very clearly delineated the informal setting in which she acquired her knowledge of local history in the following description:

> Grandma used to sit and tell things that happened; just sit and talk. Well, us kids would set down and listen, because we had nothing to turn our attention to, except listen to her talk. We had no television, no radio, nor no nothing like that, you know, to get our mind off on something else. So we'd sit and listen to her tell things that happened, and I remembered. I don't know whether my sister did or not, but I always did. I always loved to hear her talk. I'd sit down on the floor, right

by her, and she'd sit and tell me things that happened. And I remembered.[14]

Informal Conversations, Formal Occasions

Formal occasions are gatherings for a specific purpose, during which informal conversation unrelated to the central activity may take place. Any number of such occasions could be listed here, but common ones in which talk about the past is likely to go on include reunions of all kinds, club meetings, weddings, funerals, graduations, and holiday celebrations.

Given the circumstances under which people meet on such occasions, it seems natural that talk about the past should constitute a good deal of the conversation that goes on. After all, the past is usually the common bond among all those present. Reunions, for instance, are based on the celebration of the fellowship or association the participants have had with one another in years past. In addition, other occasions, especially weddings and funerals, may function as home-comings, bringing members of the family or community together, perhaps for the first time in years.

The sense of community that people share in these settings is frequently expressed in talk about the shared past: "I don't mean to speak ill of the dead, but did you hear about the time he accidentally shot his grandfather?" "Well, now, wasn't his great-grandmother the first woman sheriff the county ever had?" Reminiscences of similar formal occasions in the past may also appear in the conversation: "Remember what happened at Rachel's wedding?"

14. Mrs. Sarah Jane Koger, tape-recorded interview, Jamestown, Tennessee, June 18, 1979.

"At our tenth class reunion, Tommy Jenkins backed over a picnic bench and broke his leg!"

Formal Conversations, Formal Occasions

The third type of setting for talk about the past is the interview, whose specific purpose is to allow organized, patterned conversation, in the form of questions and answers, on historical topics. Most historical researchers who have used oral sources have relied exclusively on information gathered in interview settings, because oral sources have been used predominantly to supplement the written record, and researchers have simply conducted interviews to fill in gaps, rather than to uncover new information about undocumented aspects of the past. Yet local historians should not assume that the only way to get the kinds of oral information they need or believe to be available is by interviewing people. All the settings in which talk about the past goes on need to be exploited, for the ways people talk about the past in each setting, and, consequently, the kinds of information available in each, are different.

In both informal settings and formal settings in which informal conversation takes place, the most striking characteristic of the talk that occurs is that it flows easily and naturally from one subject to another, as one speaker after another picks up a different thread of the talk. In contrast to this kind of give-and-take among equally knowledgeable people, interviews are based on one knowledgeable person being questioned by someone else who either does not know the answers or wants to know more. Since the resulting conversation follows the course prescribed by the interviewer, rather than the person being

43

interviewed, the content of the historical information placed on tape is heavily controlled by the researcher. Yet, human memory works largely by association, and the associations that participants in informal conversations draw between persons and events can be valuable clues to the local history researcher about insiders' perceptions of or points of view about the past. A formal interview does not usually allow these kinds of associations to be drawn, thus depriving the researcher of potentially important insights into the subject at hand and the interviewee's feelings about it.

Another difference between structured interviews and informal conversations is that the topics of informal conversation are likely to be familiar to everyone present, or at least to those doing most of the talking. Because of the familiarity of the events under discussion, people often refer to some things with a catch phrase, rather than recounting them fully to an audience that has heard them before. Stories referred to by such phrases have been termed *kernel narratives* and are used most frequently among people who interact with each other on a regular basis.[15] A local history researcher working in formal and informal settings is likely to hear a good deal of historical information couched in these tantalizingly brief terms.

The local history researcher has the opportunity to broaden the heretofore limited use of oral sources by gathering information about the past in all three of the settings identified here. Researchers should, to the extent

15. Susan Kalčik uses the term *kernel narrative* in " . . . Like Ann's Gynecologist . . . : Personal Narratives in Women's Rap Groups," *Journal of American Folklore* 88 (1975): 3–11.

possible, take advantage of the informal situations in which talk about the past goes on, particularly during the early stages of research. Clearly, one cannot go around with a tape recorder in hand all the time, but a small note pad is easy to carry for jotting down items of interest to ask about later. In a situation in which historical information is likely to be exchanged, such as a reunion, a tape recorder might be introduced unobtrusively, though this should never be done secretly. Just as archival materials can be surveyed for suitable leads on a chosen topic, informal conversations about the past can be used to survey the community for knowledgeable sources of information, to compile a list of topics to be investigated (including those mentioned in kernel narratives), and generally to get a feeling for the events or kinds of events that people consider important in their community's past—all of which can serve as guides for research in formal interviews.

3

Identifying and Using Orally Communicated History

WHEN PEOPLE TALK ABOUT LOCAL HISTORY, THEY draw on a number of sources: firsthand observations of changes in the community's physical and social make-up across the years; personal experiences; conversations with other members of the community; and knowledge gleaned from all sorts of written documents and printed materials. Such a variety of sources—an enumeration by no means exhaustive—produces a broad range of topics that make up orally communicated history.

Personal Experiences

Much personal knowledge of the past is expressed in stories about events in the speaker's own experience. Although personal-experience narratives theoretically can deal with almost any topic, they tend to focus on particularly humorous, frightening, striking, or unusual occurrences, such as a narrow escape from death, an embarrassing moment, an encounter with a famous person, or an eyewitness account of a spectacular event in the community's history.

Stories about personal experiences generally focus on the speaker as the center of the action in his or her own narrative. Individual narrators are likely to have well-developed repertoires of firsthand accounts dealing with significant events in their lives. Such stories are usually highly polished from many retellings, and most tend to cast the narrator in a favorable light. Some people concentrate heavily on their personal experiences in talking about the past; the "sagamen" of Michigan's Upper Peninsula are illustrative of raconteurs who tell numerous stories in which they are the heroes of sensational exploits.[1]

Family Stories

Traditional information about a variety of episodes in a family's history is often passed from one generation to another in oral form. Such traditional knowledge often constitutes a family saga, "the body of lore that tends to cluster around families, or often the patriarchs or matriarchs of families, which is preserved . . . by oral tradition, and which is believed to be true."[2] These sagas, while varying from one family to another, are stories that frequently deal with similar themes, such as hardships on the frontier, family misfortunes, why and when grandfather migrated to the United States, the exploits of famous or

1. For examples of stories told by sagamen, see Richard M. Dorson, *Bloodstoppers and Bearwalkers: Folk Traditions from Michigan's Upper Peninsula* (Cambridge, Mass.: Harvard University Press, 1952).

2. Mody Boatright, "The Family Saga as a Form of Folklore," in *The Family Saga and Other Phases of American Folklore* (Urbana, Ill.: The University of Illinois Press, 1958), p. 1.

eccentric relatives, and the family's experiences during trying times such as wars and economic depressions.

These family stories often follow a pattern found in the narratives of other families. Their function is generally to illustrate the family's role in the community's economic, social, or political structure, or they may explain various peculiarities in the family's past, such as feuds among different branches or the fact that the family has never acquired great wealth. One type of family story recounts the family's connection with famous persons or events. For instance, a New York family tells the story of a young man who went to France in 1917 with a portion of a tricolor sash, which had belonged to Lafayette, sewn into his uniform. Lafayette had given the sash to the soldier's great-grandmother when she was thirteen, after she had delivered a warm welcome to him, in French, at a ceremony at Castle Garden in New York in 1824.[3]

Occupations

People's lives are spent largely in earning a living; thus, it is not surprising that much of what they know about the past has to do with work. Lengthy oral descriptions of processes, equipment, and daily routines can be gathered rather easily from active or retired farmers, miners, housewives, loggers, teachers, assembly line workers, physicians, railroaders, fishermen, lawyers, merchants, and so on. Disasters, tragedies, violence, and oppression are the subjects that constitute a major part of this body of narratives. Narratives about particular events associated with

3. Amos Wilder, "Between Reminiscence and History," *Massachusetts Historical Society Proceedings* 87 (1975): 114.

occupations often enter oral channels and are passed along to subsequent generations of workers. Some persons may thus have secondhand knowledge of how things were done before their time, usually from a parent or other older person.

Not all orally communicated history about occupations is grim. People may recall pranks and practical jokes played on each other in occupational settings. Medical schools, military bases, and lumberjack camps, for instance, are notorious for stories associated with sending the greenhorn on a fool's errand to find such things as a sterile Fallopian tube or a left-handed monkey wrench.

The Community's Past

Communities comprise individuals and groups of individuals who have shared historical experiences. Aspects of the past that are held in common constitute a major part of community life and thought. The sense of community is heightened when local narratives, some old and some recent, are recounted about a variety of subjects.

Local place names and landmarks. Accounts of the way a community acquired its name are often considered a part of local history, but when the name is unusual or its original meaning has been lost, the explanation may be less an example of accurate history than of folk etymology. Many place names may be nothing more than misunderstood or mispronounced words.[4]

There may be more than one story accounting for a

4. For a good discussion of this type of place-name legend, see W. F. H. Nicolaisen, "Some Humorous Folk-Etymological Narratives," *New York Folklore Quarterly* 3 (1977): 1–13.

community's name. Azusa, California, is reported to have been named by enthusiastic citizens who believed their community contained everything desirable "from A to Z in the USA"; a less imaginative but more likely explanation claims that *Azusa* was the name of the early owner of the land on which the community stands.

Both physical and cultural features of the landscape also inspire people to tell stories explaining their origins. Chalk outcroppings in parts of England, for instance, have spawned local legends accounting for their human or animal shapes. Similarly, unusual architectural features mutely encourage people to devise explanations for them. An abandoned house in Indiana, for instance, has an unusual ramp-like structure on one side. This unexplained feature has spawned unverifiable legends about its function and about previous owners of the house.[5]

Local events. In formal history, the past is portrayed as consisting of one event succeeding another in chronological order. While orally communicated history may not always adhere to the sequential order in which events transpired, it does in fact deal to a large extent with occurrences. These can range from the founding of the community, through the disasters—natural or economic—it has survived, to the latest squabble over urban renewal.

While the events and topics recounted in orally communicated history are virtually limitless, changes in the economic structure of a region or a community are of particular importance, since the coming and/or departure of an industry, for example, affects many lives in a community and is likely to be a prominent item of discussion in

5. Carol Mitchell, "The White House," *Indiana Folklore* 2 (1969): 97–109.

orally communicated history. Many points of view are set forth in these accounts by the owners and operators of the industry, the workers in the labor force and their families, area merchants, and others who are affected.

Heroes and Villains

When people tell stories about their families, their occupations, and other topics of local concern, they are likely to talk about persons as well as events, recounting people's exploits and eccentricities. These stories, while admiring, disparaging, or ridiculing the chief characters, are always told locally for truth, although they may be historically unverifiable and, in fact, be found in identical or similar form in other regions.

Heroes include such figures as successful business leaders, especially when their life stories exemplify the rags-to-riches model; abnormally strong individuals such as Strap Buckner of early Texas fame, who threw a red blanket over his shoulder and walked out on the prairie, challenging a huge black bull leading a stampede and defeating it in single combat; and native sons and daughters who made good in the world outside the home community, like Cordell Hull, who went from the Bloomington community in Pickett County, Tennessee, to Washington, D.C., where he became Franklin D. Roosevelt's secretary of state.

Villains can also serve as the subjects of anecdotes. Overbearing and cruel bosses and outlaws are perhaps the most common types. A former Cumberland River steamboat captain tells how the legendary Catty Martin, first mate during the late nineteenth century, handled the roustabouts as they unloaded cargo at the many landings on the river:

> Now, Catty Martin was a rough first mate, but probably the best ever on the river. He'd take him a bucket of coal, they said, up on the top deck and stand there and watch the roustabouts carry cargo off and on the boat. He'd cut drive with a piece of coal as big as your hand and take them rousters up against the head if one got lazy and got out of line.
>
> They's scared to death of him, but they knew where they stood with him at all times. He never had any trouble getting a replacement when one got sick or quit or something.[6]

People also recount stories of persons who failed in society's eyes and went over to the wrong side of the law. The attitudes expressed toward outcasts vary in these accounts. Sometimes they are condemned, and their acts of lawlessness and violence are regarded with horror. In other cases, the outlaw is viewed sympathetically as a romantic, Robin Hood sort of individual, or as having been wronged by the law. Jesse James and Gary Gilmore (executed in 1978) provide proof that certain personalities can be either criminals or heroes in the public mind, depending on whose viewpoint is expressed.

Such a brief sampling of the topics of orally communicated history reveals what an embarrassment of riches the local historian has to work with. It is not enough to collect these materials, however; they are simply raw data, like census records, treaties, and other written sources of history, and they need to be woven into a narrative account.

6. Captain Escar O. Coe, tape-recorded interview, Burkesville, Kentucky, February 12, 1976.

Using Oral Sources for Local History

Using oral sources in local historical research requires both judgment and imagination. Just as written documents must be weighed for accuracy and relevance, so must information gathered from oral sources. The fact that orally communicated history affords a very different kind of information about the past than that contained in records, documents, and other standard historical sources, does not excuse it from rigid and careful scrutiny appropriate to oral sources.

As stated earlier, orally communicated information about the past may be used to supplement the historical record, to complement written history, or to provide primary information about the past. For the local history researcher, the use of oral sources can range from adding flavor and intricate detail to well-documented historical subjects, to serving as the integral core of information about topics for which little written documentation exists. One's choice of a research topic will determine to some degree the extent to which oral historical information can be used. For instance, a researcher interested in the political history of a community may rely less on oral sources of information than someone concerned with the history of an immigrant group in the area, particularly one whose members have retained their native language.

Fleshing Out the Historical Record

Even when a subject is well documented in print, oral sources can be useful in filling in gaps in the record. Many oral history projects, in fact, are designed to elicit information that will supplement what is already available from written materials. For instance, certain kinds of specific information, such as the circumstantial details surrounding a memorable event in the community's past, may be garnered from firsthand, eyewitness accounts. Such reports can vary a good deal in structure and content from one narrator to another, depending on the perceptions and recollections of the individuals recounting them, but the local historian can winnow through them to piece together a relatively full, coherent, composite account of the event in question.

Eyewitness accounts can be used not only to supply factual details about an event, but also to provide information about community reactions to that event. The following eyewitness account of a 1941 sighting of the northern lights in Indiana not only describes the phenomenon, but reports on the community's interpretation of it:

> Well, the last time that I've seen northern lights that were spectacular was just before World War Two. Course, everybody says, you know, that anything phenomenal like that portends disaster, and all that sorta stuff. And everybody was wondering what terrible thing was going to happen. . . . It was so spectacular that I remember everybody was out here in the yard looking on—they'd come clear over our house there. And just like fingers. They'd stretch and then go back. It was real ghastly, really! The most spectacular I'd ever seen. But they were just yellow lights; they weren't colored. But it was real spectacular. Everybody all around was out there watching them. It was that unusual. It was in August, I think, and World War Two started then in December.[7]

In addition to specific details about an event, oral sources

---

7. Cited in Sandra K. D. Stahl, "The Personal Narrative as a Folklore Genre" (Ph.D. diss., Indiana University, 1975), p. 279.

can provide insights into the private human motivations behind the actions represented in public documents and can offer explanations for cryptic features of the written record. For instance, in a study of agricultural land ownership in an Iowa county, people's oral descriptions of customary practices, their feelings about the land, and their families' connections with particular sites accounted for the ways the land had been utilized and cared for within one generation, then passed along to the next generation as a means of perpetuating a traditional family life style. While raw historical information obtained from deeds and farm records having to do with planting and harvesting was available to indicate *how* the land had been used, only oral recollections gave the reasons behind that utilization.[8]

In addition to being used to fill in the historical records, oral sources are helpful in amplifying the sometimes scanty information available in written form: newspaper accounts and court records of murders and other sensational crimes, for example, may give only a skeletal outline of events, while oral accounts of those same occurrences may describe more fully the crimes themselves, various actions or circumstances leading up to them, legal proceedings associated with them, and community reactions to the events and their perpetrators—in short, oral accounts provide a wealth of detailed information that puts flesh on the bare bones of records and brings the events to life.

Oral sources can also be profitably used to document events that changed the course of a community's history.

8. Rebecca Conard, "The Family Farm: A Study of Folklife in Historical Context" (Paper delivered to the American Folklore Society, Los Angeles, October 1979).

Spoken accounts of school integration, for instance, can provide information about political maneuverings among various community groups, the personal concern of parents for their children's well-being during the integration process, the emotional involvement with issues at hand that strained and sometimes destroyed friendships and disrupted other social relationships—all of the feelings and ferment surrounding the affair that were not reported in the newspapers or other contemporary accounts. Economic factors in a community's make-up may also be documented more fully by utilizing oral information. Research on prominent industries and occupations can be further documented by interviewing a range of people involved with them, from corporate executives to blue-collar workers and their families. Consider, for example, how many lives are affected when a Pennsylvania coal miner's union goes out on strike, when logging and rafting operations are terminated on a river in Maine, and when the Boeing Aircraft Corporation of Seattle is awarded a government contract. The local historian may broaden the scope of research immeasurably by obtaining and representing as many viewpoints as possible, indicating which ones seem predominant in the community and which are in the minority. Always, it is well to remember that issues closely affecting people's lives may be extremely sensitive and emotionally charged and that handling them will require great tact on the part of the researcher.[9]

9. See Kenneth S. Goldstein's "Ethnographic Dynamite," in his *Guide for Field Workers in Folklore* (Hatboro, Pa.: Folklore Associates, 1964), pp. 116–117.

The Human Side of History

While written documents supply factual information about the whys and wherefores of important events and movements, orally communicated history often expresses how people felt about those events, how they reacted to them, and how the events affected their lives. Eyewitness accounts of historical occurrences often provide this human dimension by reporting not only the details of what happened, but the emotional responses of individuals to the event itself, as revealed in the following oral account:

> The Gradyville Flood happened one summer, July 7, 1907. One stormy afternoon a big cloud arose full of lightning, flashes of lightning everywhere. We became deeply concerned because our father was away from home with two horses pulling a buggy, and a man was helping him with his work. When he came, the man got out and took his bags out, and the man who was looking after the horses went to the barn. It was about six o'clock when they came, but he didn't leave the barn until after nine o'clock, because the rain was so heavy.
>
> The next morning, we learned that the town of Gradyville had washed away in the flood. There were twenty-one who lost their lives; houses were blown away, torn away. The stream filled up so fast that they couldn't get out of the water. The only place that was left was the Wilmore Hotel, which was operated by Mr. Jim Wilmore, who was the manager of a store there in the town. But his mother and sister, who lived on a little island in the river bed, were both washed away and killed by it.
>
> It was such a tragedy. Now, I witnessed this because my father took us children to see the effect of the flood, and what had been damaged, and to attend the funeral of twin boys who were drowned—the Wilmore boys, I believe they were.
>
> I heard one of my neighbors say that, when she was just three or four years old, she had some visitors, some children

playing with her, and her mother put them up on top of the table in their kitchen to keep them from being washed away when the flood broke into their house. . . .
I shall never forget the flashes of lightning. This, and as water poured on our back porch, mother and us two children would sweep the water off the porch as much as we could to keep it from blowing into the kitchen under the door.[10]

Personal experience narratives of historical events, told by individuals directly involved in the action described in the story, are often gripping human documents. A veteran of the trench warfare of World War I, for example, described his initial experience at the front this way:

I was in the front line of combat in 1918. I traveled through row after row of large cannons. Guns and big shells were stacked nearby—miles and miles of them, to be used in the opening battle. Things were quiet, and all of a sudden those guns all fired at once. It was 1:00 A.M. in the morning; then, at daylight, the command was given: "Over the top!" Everybody was ordered to go forward, with bayonets fixed, and machine guns begin to chatter and we charged into the German lines, which was about two hundred yards from us. We leaped into the trenches where the German soldiers were. They were well equipped with machine guns, rifles, grenades, and so forth. The battle was on. It was awful! Men dying all around me by the hundreds with bullets and bayonets. I was a Christian and I prayed all the time, "Lord, make it possible so I don't have to kill anyone." As I went forward, every German soldier I met threw down his gun and surrendered.[11]

10. Mary Lucy Lowe, tape-recorded interview, Columbia, Kentucky, December 5, 1978, as part of the Lake Cumberland Library District Oral History Project, Burkesville, Kentucky. The original tape is on deposit at the Kentucky Historical Society Library, Frankfort.
11. Willie Standridge, Archive of Folklore, Folklife, and Oral History, Western Kentucky University, Bowling Green, Kentucky, unaccessioned tape.

Orally communicated history can reveal the human side of the past also by showing how historical events— international, national, or local—can dramatically change the course of an individual's life. One such account comes from Edwin Ettinger of San Clemente, California, who recalled that he first heard news of the attack on Pearl Harbor in 1941 while visiting in the home of a Canadian friend who had "a very pretty sister." If Mr. Ettinger's life had not been disrupted by the entry of the United States into World War II, he says, tongue in cheek, to his children, "You might have had another mother."[12] Personal narratives like these serve to bring international events into the scope of local history and help to fix the dates of events in people's minds.

Events on a local level can also precipitate a traumatic alteration in life styles. The construction of a dam or a highway, for instance, often necessitates the removal of several families or even entire communities. When people's roots are generations deep in the land from which they are evicted, the psychological impact cannot be compensated for in terms of the property's market value, and the uprooted ones' grief and bitterness may be clearly expressed in their oral recollections of the event.[13]

Everyday Aspects of the Past

Written history of all kinds—whether on the interna-

12. Edwin Ettinger, tape-recorded interview, San Clemente, California, July 4, 1977.

13. For an apparent example of psychic trauma that ended in the death of a West Virginia woman who was eighty-nine when the notice came for her to move from her ancestral home because of dam construction, see Michael Meador, "Aunt Nannie Meador and the Bluefield Dam," *Goldenseal* 6 (1980): 24–30.

tional, national, or local level—typically deals with wars, elections, inventions, depressions, disasters, and other events that change the course of history.[14] Despite the fact that important historical occurrences may be better understood when they are placed within the context of the typical conditions under which life was lived, the routines and activities of everyday life—the background against which "history" takes place—have generally been neglected by most formal historians. The lack of descriptions of ordinary people doing ordinary things gives us very little idea of what the past was like for the people who lived through it, leaving us to wonder, "While the papers were full of news about the Spanish-American war, what was on the mind of the Pennsylvania Dutch farm wife?"[15]

Admittedly, there is little written information to go on in documenting the everyday aspect of the past, aside from random letters, diaries, and travel accounts; but orally communicated information about what people "used to do" can help to fill that void by documenting a variety of subjects that may be only hinted at in written source material—such subjects as childhood pastimes; family life; courting customs and other social patterns; occupational

14. Notable exceptions to this statement are the works produced by European and American social and cultural historians in the past fifty years, including, among others, Marc Bloch's *French Rural History: An Essay on Its Basic Characteristics* (Berkeley: University of California Press, 1970); Lucian Febvre's *A New Kind of History: From the Writings of Lucian Febvre* (New York: Harper and Row, 1973); Edward P. Thompson's *The Making of the English Working Class* (New York: Pantheon Books, 1964); Philip J. Greven's *Four Generations: Population, Land, and Family in Colonial America* (Ithaca: Cornell University Press, 1970); and Stephan Thernstrom's *Poverty and Progress: Social Mobility in a Nineteenth-Century City* (Cambridge: Harvard University Press, 1964).

15. Henry Glassie, "A Folkloristic Thought on the Promise of Oral History," in *Selections from the Fifth and Sixth National Colloquia on Oral History* (New York: Oral History Association, 1972), p. 56.

routines and leisure-time activities; methods of procuring, preserving, and preparing food; bartering and other economic practices. Using the oral recollections of older residents, George E. Evans, a British cultural historian, has produced an admirable series of books documenting the pretechnological period of history in traditionally agricultural areas of northeastern England. Many of his informants dwelled at length on the everyday aspects of life in the past.[16]

Often these accounts of typical activities offer an explanation as well as a description of social customs. Mary and Russell Emery of Silver Lake, Oregon, for instance, tell how women used to pack up their children for overnight visits with neighbors in the lonely desert country of south-central Oregon:

> "The womenfolks," said Mrs. Emery, "they'd go visit one of the other families when the men were off working, and they'd load their kids in their buggy and go stay all night with them."
>
> "Stay two, three days," added her husband. "I remember [once] Mrs. Owsley over here called up my mother, said 'Will's gone. Wish you'd come over and stay all night with me. I'm afraid to stay alone.' So my mother, she loaded Jim and I on a horse and she got on another horse and we rode across the hill there and stayed all night."[17]

This reminiscence provides not only a succinct description

---

16. Evans's *The Days That We Have Seen* (London: Faber and Faber, 1975) is representative of his fine work. Paul Thompson argues, in *Voices from the Past: Oral History* (Oxford: Oxford University Press, 1978), that "the richest possibilities for oral history lie within the development of more socially conscious and democratic history" (p. x).

17. Russell Emery and Mary Emery, tape-recorded interview, Silver Lake, Oregon, August 8, 1978.

of the turn-of-the-century custom of overnight visiting among women in that part of Oregon, but gives the reason behind it, as well—namely, to relieve women's apprehensions and anxieties during their husbands' absences from home. Information of that sort is available only from oral accounts.

The element of the ordinary or typical in the past can also be documented by recording the life histories of individuals. By life histories we do not mean simply bare-bones identification of the major events in people's lives—where and to whom they were born, whom they married, where they were educated and employed—but comprehensive, detailed accounts of the various stages of their lives. The premise behind collecting and analyzing a life history is that any individual is in many respects typical of the society and culture in which he or she lives. The life-history researcher may not come across information pertaining to every facet of community life and thought in the study of one individual, but will assuredly tap into every major current. Thus, through orally recorded life histories of ordinary citizens, as well as outstanding ones, an entire historical era or geographical region may be portrayed.[18]

Materials for life histories must be elicited primarily

18. Examples of publications based on life histories include Dorothy Gallagher, *Hannah's Daughters: Six Generations of an American Family, 1876–1976* (New York: Thomas Y. Crowell, 1976); Theodore Rosengarten [and Nate Shaw], *All God's Dangers: The Life of Nate Shaw* (New York: Alfred A. Knopf, 1974); Rev. C. C. White and Ada Morehead Holland, *No Quittin' Sense* (Austin: University of Texas Press, 1969); Roger E. Mitchell, *I'm a Man That Works: The Biography of Don Mitchell of Merrill, Maine* (Orono, Me.: Northeast Folklore Society, 1978); William Couch, *These Are Our Lives* (Chapel Hill: University of North Carolina Press, 1939); and Tom Terrill and Jerrold Hirsch, *Such As Us* (Chapel Hill: University of North Carolina Press, 1978).

through oral interviews with the person whose life is being documented and the information then patched together into proper chronological sequence.

A Community's Unrecorded Past

Additional uses for oral sources are in documenting whole areas of a community's history for which written records are missing or are incomplete.[19] For instance, cottage industries, such as basket-making, furniture-making, and other traditional crafts, which once were the economic mainstay for many families, leave behind no written traces in the form of business ledgers or tax records. Yet the people involved in those industries can provide richly detailed oral descriptions of these pursuits and can indicate the extent to which the entire community depended on them economically. Similarly, there are instances in which an entire community may have left virtually no formal record of its existence, and its past must be reconstructed almost entirely from oral recollections of former residents and other individuals familiar with the community.[20]

The local historian accustomed to formal documentation may find the suggested uses of oral sources set forth here, as well as concepts and procedures for dealing with

19. An excellent example of this kind of research is Charles W. Joyner's *Slave Folklife: Antebellum Black Culture in the South Carolina Low Country* (Urbana: University of Illinois Press, forthcoming), based largely on the oral recollections and traditions of former slaves and their descendants and on legends, tales, proverbs, and songs circulating in the community he studied.

20. William Lynwood Montell's *Saga of Coe Ridge: A Study in Oral History* (Knoxville: University of Tennessee Press, 1970) is an example of the reconstruction of a community's history based on oral sources.

them, quite different from textbook methodologies. That should not keep anyone from utilizing orally communicated history, however, for the end product is certainly worth the trouble it takes. Relevant oral information, always available to the diligent researcher, will help to make any historical account more complete.

4

Testing Oral Sources for Historical Validity

RESEARCHERS INTERESTED IN THE HISTORY OF families, communities, and ethnic groups frequently find that too few written documents remain intact to permit reconstruction of the past from standard sources. When newspaper files, court records, and other written sources normally utilized by historians have been destroyed by fire, flood, thievery, political chicanery, and simple neglect, the only remaining source materials may be the oral recollections and personal reminiscences of local people. Despite the general hesitance of formal historians to analyze and use oral sources of historical information, a handful of folklorists, anthropologists, and ethnohistorians have recognized the usefulness of the tape recorder as a means of reaching into the lives and minds of individuals from every walk of life to document the past. These researchers have come to realize that oral tradition is often the only available source of historical information, especially for American Indians and regional and ethnic groups, and that comprehensive and meaningful history can be written only when oral sources are researched as thoroughly as written ones.

Many local historians, like their academic counterparts, continue to hold the erroneous notion that "old people's recollections are notoriously fallible," and that oral historical expression springs up only "whenever trustworthy records are not available."[1] The question of the validity of orally communicated history has commanded the attention of folklorists, anthropologists, and historians for the past half-century.[2] Historians who have doubts about the reliability and accuracy of the spoken word feel that the human memory is incapable of retaining a firm grip on historical facts and that historical truth becomes distorted and diluted through repeated retellings. They point out that oral accounts of historical events not only vary in important details, but may even be contradictory. How can

1. Homer C. Hockett, *The Critical Method in Historical Research and Writing* (New York: Macmillan, 1955), pp. 49–51. A softening of this harsh position among formal historians was apparent in the panel on the historical content of orally communicated history at the 1970 meeting of the American Historical Association. The papers presented there were published in a special issue of the *Journal of the Folklore Institute* 8 (1971).

2. Arguments for and against the use of oral sources of historical information fall into four basic categories, extending from the totally negative outlook to the totally positive: (1) All orally communicated history is false and should be avoided; (2) orally communicated history, although neatly embellished, does not always make havoc of historical fact; (3) orally communicated history mirrors formal history and may be profitably employed to shed light on social, cultural, and popular aspects of the past; and (4) all orally communicated history is rooted in historical fact. Richard M. Dorson approached the question of the veracity of oral recollections in a 1964 article, "The Debate over the Trustworthiness of Oral Traditional History," reprinted in *Folklore: Selected Essays* (Bloomington, Ind.: Indiana University Press, 1972), pp. 199–223. Dorson focused on American Indian oral historical materials, buttressing his arguments with additional materials from Polynesia and Iceland.

such flagrantly inconsistent sources be considered a valid historical record?

The argument that the human memory cannot be trusted has been disproved by research among groups of people around the world who have a marked propensity for retaining historical truths over long periods of time. Ethnohistorians have demonstrated the veracity of orally communicated history among American Indians, Africans, and South Asian groups whose cultures are overwhelmingly oral and rich in ancient historical traditions. Studies in these areas indicate that, while orally communicated history thrives best in a nonliterate culture, it is preserved with considerable accuracy under certain favorable social and cultural conditions. The Icelandic family sagas, for instance, were transmitted orally for hundreds of years among a people who had lived for generations in one place, who had strong emotional identification with familiar landmarks, and who trained young people with a propensity for storytelling in the art of the saga.[3]

Even in literate, industrialized Europe and America, it is possible to find individuals who have received and nurtured oral historical traditions that transcend three, four, five, and even six generations. One of the most convincing cases for the accuracy of orally communicated history has been made by writer Alex Haley, who tapped into centuries-old genealogical traditions of his own family in his search for his West African progenitors. That Haley's findings were no fluke is demonstrated by the following

---

3. Knut Liestøl, *The Origin of the Icelandic Family Sagas* (Oslo: H. Aschehoug and Company, 1930).

oral genealogical account from a thirteen-year-old black girl in Mississippi:

> My family history goes—well, as far as I know, it goes all the way back to 1700. 1700: Sarah Martha Blakeman was born. She wasn't a slave then. 1731: She was thirty years old; she was captured for a slave. She'd already given birth to Sarah Marie Blakeman. That's my great-great-great-grandmother. Sarah Marie Blakeman then gave birth to my great-great-grandmother, Martha Blakeman, who was a part of the Freedom Train [Underground Railroad]. Then *she* gave birth to my great-grandmother, who just died lately, Sarah Marie Blakeman II; and my great-grandmother just told me the story. And my uncle and my great-great-grandmother took part in the Freedom Train. They escaped, but he got scared, and he turned back, but he was killed. My great-great-grandmother walked across the bridge of freedom. I've forgot what year that was in. And not long ago, my great-grandmother died. She was ninety-two.

The girl explained how the information had been preserved in her family:

> It was passed down the generations. Each time someone was born, about the time they got about twelve, they [were] told. And I'm supposed to pass it on through a generation when I get older. . . . The daughter passes the word down.[4]

Not all orally communicated history on the local level, of course, will have the time depth of that example. Yet an alert researcher will encounter people who can recount historical traditions they received from their grandparents. Such source material is potentially of great value to local history, but it must be weighed as historical evidence

4. Tape-recorded interview, Bentonia, Mississippi, January 28, 1980. The name *Blakeman* is a pseudonym for the surname identified by the informant.

before being included as a valid part of a documented written narrative. Even firsthand accounts—as opposed to those that have been transmitted over several generations—need to be subjected to effective tests for validity.

Two kinds of tests can be applied to oral sources of historical information: internal tests, which evaluate the material in terms of its own self-consistency; and external tests, which compare and contrast oral information with written accounts and physical evidence.[5]

Internal Tests for Validity

Identifying Folklore Themes

In using oral sources for historical reconstruction, local historians need to understand and appreciate the way in which floating themes and motifs move with fluidity and ease from one story to another to lend color to a given account. Many recurrent folklore themes and motifs are identified in reference works that have been utilized by folklorists for years. A comprehensive general reference

5. In 1961, Richard M. Dorson prepared a contract research report for the Indian Land Claims Commission of the Department of Justice, titled "The Historical Validity of Oral Tradition." In that document, he suggested certain criteria for evaluating the veracity of oral traditions of Indian land claims, including the identification of folklore themes grafted onto historical settings, allowance for personal and ethnocentric bias, cross-checking multiple traditions, corroboration of traditions from printed records, corroboration of traditions from geographical landmarks, corroboration of traditions from material culture, and a personal knowledge of the character of the informant. Dorson's criteria were later applied to a body of traditional Scottish narratives in "Sources for the Traditional History of the Scottish Highlands and Western Islands," *Journal of the Folklore Institute* 8 (1971): 147–184.

work employed in documenting universal motifs is the revised edition of Stith Thompson's six-volume *Motif-Index of Folk Literature*, published by Indiana University Press between 1955 and 1958. In preparing this monumental work, Thompson gleaned thousands of traditional motifs (striking narrative units recurring in two or more texts) from published collections of oral materials. Although the work is worldwide in scope, emphasis is placed on European and North American sources. Bibliographic references to each motif indicate where it can be found in published and archival collections. While no one section of the *Motif-Index* deals exclusively with historical materials, the judicious researcher can find, scattered throughout, many items that occur repeatedly in historical legends of one variety or another. The following examples from the Thompson index include motifs that we have encountered in collecting narratives about local history:

D1318.5.2	The corpse bleeds when murderer touches it.
E4221.1.11.5.1(e)	Ineradicable bloodstain.
F617	Mighty wrestler.
F624.3	Strong man lifts cart.
X940 (am)	Strong man lifts tree ten men have failed to budge.
X981 (ch)	Man rolls barrel downhill, putting pistol bullet through bunghole each time it comes around.
X1523.2	Lies about farming on steep mountain.

In 1966, Ernest Warren Baughman expanded Thompson's index by including many additional motifs from the British Isles and North America in a one-volume *Type and Motif-Index of the Folktales of England and North America*, published by the Humanities Press in 1966. The

Baughman index is the best bet for finding scattered motifs contained in oral historical narrative texts.

Another index folklorists find useful is Stith Thompson's *The Types of the Folktale,* revised edition, brought out in 1961 by Suomalainen Tiedakatemia (Academia Scientiarum Fennical, Helsinki), but in its stress on animal stories and fairy tales, *The Types of the Folktale* excludes consideration of legends of all varieties. There is, however, a section on jokes and anecdotes that contains bibliographic references to humorous yarns about numbskulls, parsons and religious orders, married couples, individuals, and liars. These kinds of stories are often told as truth about eccentric characters in a family or community. Consulting Thompson's tale-type index may save a local historian from printing a story for truth just because it was told about a local figure.

In their migration from one geographical area to another, traditional narratives and motifs frequently acquire the names of local persons and places in the process of relocation.[6] Yet, since the basic elements of plot remain relatively stable, such narratives and motifs can be categorized. Certain legend indexes prepared as finding lists for folklorists may be of help to the local historian.[7]

Countless historical legends told and heard as true have been published, often in obscure books and journals. Regrettably, no index exists that identifies and classifies them

6. Examples of these migratory narratives are presented in Appendix B.

7. Chief among such indexes are Reidar Th. Christiansen's *The Migratory Legends* (Helsinki: Suomalainen Tiedakatemia, 1958); Barbara Allen Woods's *The Devil in Dog Form: A Partial Type-Index of Devil Legends* (Berkeley: University of California Press, 1959); and Byrd Howell Granger's *A Motif Index of Lost Mines and Treasure Legends* (Tucson: University of Arizona Press, 1978).

according to plot and action; much valuable work remains to be done in this regard. In the meantime, local historians seeking to document oral items that they suspect to be migratory should search through publications containing bodies of regional and topical legends.[8] Through the process of identifying these floating narrative elements, the local historical researcher can peel away the embellishmental husk to reveal the historical kernels of truth. Because the folkloristic parts of an oral historical account are incidental to and independent of the facts surrounding the actual event, "if it were possible to remove all traces of the folkloristic elements from the account, the basic historical document with its facts would remain substantially unchanged from the historian's point of view."[9] While the resulting oral historical account would be a complete and usable document, it would be a far poorer one with the colorful elements removed. The function of these elements in orally communicated history seems to be to ensure that the event does not slip out of oral circulation with the passing of the oldest living witness to it. Take, as a case in point, the following Kentucky ghost story, which

8. Titles that bear looking at in this connection include J. Frank Dobie, *Legends of Texas* (Dallas: Southern Methodist University Press, 1924); Richard M. Dorson, *Bloodstoppers and Bearwalkers: Folk Traditions of Michigan's Upper Peninsula* (Cambridge, Mass.: Harvard University Press, 1952); Richard M. Dorson, *Jonathan Draws the Long Bow: New England Popular Tales and Legends* (Cambridge, Mass.: Harvard University Press, 1946); Charles S. Neely, *Tales and Songs of Southern Illinois* (Menasha, Wisc.: George Banta Publishing Company, 1938); Austin Fife and Alta Fife, *Saints of Sage and Saddle: Folklore among the Mormons* (Bloomington, Ind.: Indiana University Press, 1956); and Reuben A. Long and E. R. Jackman, *The Oregon Desert* (Caldwell, Ida.: Caxton Printers, 1964).

9. Richard Hurst, "History and Folklore," *New York Folklore Quarterly* 25 (1969): 252.

contains accurate genealogical details, partial description of a house, and mention of several social customs and practices:

"Big" Ransie Rasner—we always called him Pa Rasner—had a brother, Ben, who lived in this old log house above the Bray Graveyard—about a mile from the graveyard on toward Rock Bridge.

Pa had another brother, lived out near Palm Garden, over close to the Glasgow road. That was Bill. Well, Bill got up early one morning and was going to walk the four or five miles across there to Ben's house and help Ben cut and shock wheat—trade out work with him. Had his hounds with him.

They always said the Bray Graveyard was haunted. I've heard the old people tell about hearing and seeing things there. Anyway, Bill and them dogs were passing by the graveyard, and it was still dark. Said something white floated across the road in front of them and disappeared into that graveyard. Said his dogs had been running down the road in front of him until that thing floated across the road. Said them dogs were scared to death; they begin whining and walking right beside Bill. Said he couldn't walk for them.

He went on down to Ben's house, and it was just breaking day. Said he laid down in the open breezeway of the house to wait for his brother to get up, and the dogs laid down right beside him. Wouldn't move; afraid to.

They never did know what that thing was.[10]

When the story is stripped of its supernatural motifs, the following items of historical interest remain:

1. The custom of distinguishing between two members in the same family with identical names by using diminutive and superlative prefixes is alluded to: there was another

---

10. Willie Montell, pencil-and-pad interview, Rock Bridge, Monroe County, Kentucky, November 26, 1977.

member of the Rasner family who went by the name of "Little" Ransie.
2. The house was constructed of logs and had an open breezeway. We recognize a dogtrot house by this description.
3. The Bray Cemetery, which still exists, is identified by name.
4. The custom of swapping labor among members of the family and community is mentioned, as is the practice of cutting and shocking wheat by hand.
5. The pack of hounds indicates that Bill Rasner was a hunter, either for pleasure or subsistence or both.
6. People of the community engaged in storytelling sessions in which ghost narratives were exchanged.

Take away the four basic folklore motifs—E332.2 (h), "Ghost seen on road at night"; E334.2, "Ghost haunts burial spot"; E421.1.3.1, "Ghost visible to dogs"; and E422.4.3, "Ghost in white," and there is nothing sensational about the facts surrounding the event; Bill Rasner's trip to help his brother represented just another day of routine work in the family's history and offered little to guarantee its oral remembrance and continuance through time. But add the element of the supernatural, with attendant ghostlore motifs, and witness the creation of an interesting story, alive and viable a century later.

Collating Divergent Accounts

Rarely is one single informant able to recount all details surrounding a specific event of years ago. But when enough people are interviewed, trends develop, patterns unfold, and truth emerges. By gathering an ample number of oral accounts describing an event, the historian can likely discern the truth of the matter. While nine separate narrations about the same incident cannot each be accepted as accurate rendering of history, they can be placed side by side and analyzed to discern the basic common thread involved. For the sections of the accounts where there is agreement among all nine informants, the local historian can, without too much hesitance, accept these as factual history. If, for example, all accounts told about a murder mention the same murderer and victim, that portion of the oral accounts can be accepted as fact.

Divergent accounts are not necessarily in disagreement with each other, although they may sometimes seem to be, on the surface. A case in point is the seemingly contradictory accounts of the lynching of the McDonald Boys in Menominee, Michigan. One oral account maintained that the bodies were strung up on a railroad crossing; another said that the gallows had been a pine tree. Only when old photographs turned up, showing the bodies hanging from both places, was it determined that the McDonalds had been lowered from the railroad sign, dragged to the tree, and hoisted up again.[11]

Each oral account represents truth as known by its narrator. A close analysis of each text will often demonstrate that it represents that portion of the story with which the narrator could naturally identify through personal or ancestral association. For example, Bill Poindexter of Ashlock, Kentucky, claimed that only his father was willing to go to the black colony on Coe Ridge to get the body of Will Taylor, Poindexter's neighbor, whose throat had been

11. Richard M. Dorson, "The Oral Historian and the Folklorist," in *Selections from the Fifth and Sixth National Colloquia on Oral History* (New York: Oral History Association, 1972), p. 48.

slashed by one of the black residents. Other oral traditions stated that Will Taylor's own family members went for the corpse. What actually happened was that, when Taylor's family made preparations to go for the body, they asked their neighbors to accompany them; only Poindexter responded to their request.[12]

Allowing for Embellishment

Incidental details used in describing historical events and personalities must be evaluated with extreme caution. Narratives about local history may contain a certain amount of coloration, which makes incidents they describe more memorable. Such embellishmental detail does not take away from the historical core of truth, however, because such improvisations are usually concerned mainly with nonessential details. It is during the process of coloration that universal folklore motifs and floating legends are occasionally called upon to make a good story even better.

A fine example of the process of embellishment is the story of the attempted elopement of two white women with two black men from the Coe colony in 1889. The four had gone to Glasgow, Kentucky, to board a train for Indiana. They were already on the train when local law officials apprehended them. Up to this point in the story, the oral accounts are fairly consistent with each other, but the arrest scene has proved to be quite elastic in oral tradition. The arrest came when the white skin of one of the women was inadvertently revealed. Various accounts claim that one of the girls' gloves fell down, or a bee got

12. William Lynwood Montell, *The Saga of Coe Ridge: A Study in Oral History* (Knoxville: University of Tennessee Press, 1970), p. 195.

under her veil, or the wind blew the veil up, or she raised the veil to scratch her face. However it occurred, her identity as a white woman was revealed. Other than that one variable in the story, the oral accounts all confirmed that the two men were jailed in Glasgow to await trial, while the two women were placed on a stage and returned to their homes.

For historical purposes, it does not matter how the discovery that the women were white was made; as a consequence, informants have made free with this particular episode, using the visual image of a flash of white skin as the exciting pivotal point of the story.

The Logical Nature of Tradition

Among the basic questions the researcher should ask in analyzing oral historical sources is whether or not the information provided in a given text is logical. Granted, all of us will have occasional problems in answering that question to our satisfaction, and there may be times when the answer could go either way. Among various illogical accounts that have actually found their way into local history publications is a story claiming that wolves got into a frontier family's flock of sheep and interbred with them to the extent that a new bloodline of wolflike sheep resulted.

The migratory narratives mentioned earlier can be plausible enough to give the local historian pause over the question of their rationality. A good example is the often-published account of the frontier heroine who eludes a pursuing panther by taking off items of her clothing and tossing them in the path of the animal, which stops momentarily to sniff each one, thus permitting the woman to maintain a safe distance between them and eventually reach safety. Examining oral evidence for logical consistency may prevent an eager or naive researcher from publishing illogical material simply because it is told as truth.

Conformity with Established Historical Facts

While oral sources can frequently illuminate, add to, or even alter our understanding of written history, orally communicated information that disregards or contradicts established historical facts must be largely discounted in terms of accuracy. An oral tradition in southern Kentucky, for instance, states that the Mulkey Church near Tompkinsville was established by a group of pioneers from South Carolina in 1765 (Daniel Boone was not in the area exploring until 1769). The church could not have been established before 1798, however, for documented history records that Mulkey and his followers were located in east Tennessee until 1797. (A check into this erroneous "oral" legend uncovered the fact that a newspaper editor had fabricated much of the story in the 1930s, set it in print, and even succeeded in getting the year 1765 placed on "official" brochures and post cards.)

Another example of oral information that flies in the face of historical truth is a story from Texas claiming that a New England ancestor moved to the Lone Star State during the Civil War to help slaves escape to Canada via the Underground Railroad. Aside from the lack of evidence for the operation of the Underground Railroad in Texas, the proximity of Mexico as a potential asylum for escaped slaves makes it a more logical destination than Canada. While accounts like these have no basis in historical fact, they may have redeeming value for the local historian who uses them to illuminate community values and attitudes, without making a claim for their veracity.

Evaluating Oral Sources

In evaluating oral evidence, the sources of that evidence must be carefully considered. Which accounts are based on personal experience and which are second- or thirdhand reports? While firsthand accounts are by no means infallible, they are generally more reliable than those derived from hearsay.

When dealing with divergent accounts, it may be useful to evaluate various texts in terms of the track records of individual informants. The testimony of a contributor who is consistently and conscientiously accurate in recounting oral historical information may be judged more reliable than that of other sources whose memories have proven to be poor.

It bears repeating that most people keep historical time in perspective by dating happenings in association with regional or national events, or with occurrences or stages in their own lives. They simply do not retain dates in their minds. While the general rule of thumb in using oral sources is to suspect any date that is offered orally, some people do remember dates accurately and with ease, such as the man who gave the following account of a local lake that periodically went dry:

> . . . the lake went dry the first time in 1917, I guess. It was completely dry in 1918. . . . And, of course, the two reservoirs . . . have held back the run-off that would have gone into the lake, and that's one of the reasons it's been dry so

much since then. However, we had wet years from 1948 through 1954—well, really through 1956, in which the lake was entirely filled up again. And since then, there's been numerous dry years, and by 1959 it was completely dry, and it's only had a little dab of water in it ever since.[13]

The testimony of such persons may be used with a considerable degree of assurance. (This is all the more true for nonliterate groups who have had to rely exclusively on oral tradition for conveying history.)

Finally, the circumstances under which the evidence has been gathered need to be taken into account in weighing the information. Was the informant under any sort of duress? Was there sufficient trust established between the informant and the researcher, if the information was collected during an interview? Knowing as much as possible about one's sources of information, including the factors outlined here, will provide a solid basis for their evaluation.

Allowing for Personal and Group Bias

Most people from whom oral information about the past is gathered are willing, even eager, to relate what they know to the local historian in order to have their community's history preserved. As a result, they strive to convey their historical knowledge as accurately and as fully as possible. Yet oral accounts of historical events necessarily express the personal viewpoints of the individuals from whom they are collected, and reflect the over-all perspective on the events of the community at large. As a result, orally communicated history is as subject to bias as written

13. Forest Stratton, tape-recorded interview, Silver Lake, Oregon, July 8, 1978.

materials, such as newspaper editorials or accounts of military or economic conflicts penned by partisans. While informants normally do not deliberately falsify information, personal or community prejudices may alter an individual's interpretation and, hence, recounting of an event. Rather than consciously distorting the truth, people may gloss over details that reflect unfavorably on their own families or on other persons living in the area, or they may simply evade questions about particular subjects. In using oral sources, then, the local historian who can identify the underlying biases will be in a better position to evaluate the testimony for accuracy.

External Tests

Corroboration from Material Culture

Physical objects and cultural artifacts used in daily life during an earlier period may assist in verifying an oral tradition. For instance, the introduction to a Scottish folktale from the sixteenth century contained a detailed description of a laird's dwelling in the reign of James VI, which was corroborated 250 years later, when collector John Dewar observed the structure.[14] The ruins of buildings and statues, and the visual presence of guns and ancient armor, certain farming tools, and other handcrafted artifacts, all help to keep traditions alive. They provide the tradition-bearers of each new generation tangible substance on which to hang some of the stories in their repertoires.

14. Dorson, "Sources," pp. 183–184.

Cultural artifacts are especially helpful in keeping first-person experiences alive and talked about in family circles. A friend of ours has a flint marble that he fashioned with his own hands, as a child. Mention the marble, and he will tell of the time when he and his brother were jointly making marbles and almost killed their sister by accident. The process of making marbles is invariably part of his narrative. The cultural artifact thus binds the account of the craft process with the episode of the near-disastrous accident.

Corroborating Tradition from Continuation in Same Area

The United States abounds in local historical legends. Indeed, they may be this country's most characteristic type of oral narrative. Stories of colonial and frontier times, slavery, the Civil War, homesteading, and so on, are commonly told in family and community circles. For instance, Champ Ferguson was a Confederate guerrilla who operated in six or eight counties along the Kentucky-Tennessee state line during the Civil War. He was eventually tried, convicted, and hanged for his crimes in Nashville. We have recorded numerous accounts of his activities from people who heard the stories from their parents and grandparents. The mere fact that historical legends are still told does not make them historically accurate, of course, but that such recollections are collectible from persons who grew up in the cultural milieu in which the tales are passed along by word of mouth lends considerable credence to the possibility that these accounts may contain at least a core of truth.

Corroborating Tradition through Ethnic or Racial Groups

The historical traditions of a group are usually known and passed along orally only among the group's members. Seldom do historical traditions cross ethnic boundaries. For these reasons, the trustworthiness of an oral historical tradition is a sure bet when it is present in the repertoires of more than one group within the community, whether or not disruptive social factors are present that may tend to cause each group to be biased in its opinions of the others.

Corroboration from Printed Records

Newspaper accounts, court records, census schedules, diary entries by eyewitnesses, and a host of other printed sources may prove useful in verifying oral traditional accounts.[15] For example, Vermont's cold summer of 1816 is remembered for the bitter cold accompanied by more than ten inches of snow in June. Some people froze to death, oral accounts claim; others committed suicide through fear that the sun was cooling off. The sheep had just been sheared, but some were saved when their fleeces were tied to their freshly-shorn bodies. The beech trees did not put out their leaves again that year, and had it not been for boiled nettles, wild turnips, and hedgehogs, thousands of residents would have perished from lack of food.

While few Vermonters bothered to write about that disastrous year, these bits of oral traditional history have been corroborated by sparse contemporary printed sources

15. For a full consideration of the use of printed sources in corroboration, see Edward D. Ives, "Common Man Biography," in *Folklore Today* (Bloomington, Ind.: Indiana University Press, 1976), pp. 251–264.

in the form of diaries, newspapers, and incomplete climatologists' reports. That summer was indeed a cold one, these sources say, and history accords it the distinction of being the coldest summer on record. The cold front, accompanied by snow and blizzard conditions, struck with lightning swiftness, killing field and fruit crops, and causing great suffering to livestock. No one died, but large numbers of people went hungry. Oral traditional history surrounding Vermont's cold summer of 1816 is thus corroborated by the printed record, but the oral source, as is characteristic of orally communicated history, provides a greater store of vividly detailed information about the event than is contained in official documents.[16]

Corroboration from Accounts in Regional
Historical Literature

Local oral historical tradition may claim that slave-breeding or range wars took place in the local area. Where oral accounts exist side by side with available printed descriptions, the specific details of the local account may not be validated, but we can safely assume that slave-breeding or range wars did exist locally, otherwise they would not be a part of the local legend repertoire.

Using printed sources to corroborate oral information—especially when the materials in print are well known—may be a circular proposition, for people may have gained the information they impart orally from those printed sources. Furthermore, lack of corroboration from a printed source does not automatically invalidate orally derived

16. T. D. Seymour Bassett, "The Cold Summer of 1816 in Vermont," *New England Galaxy* 14 (1973): 15–19.

information; much of that information never appears in written form.

It may prove profitable at this point to focus on a series of oral texts surrounding the Logsdon hanging, presented in Appendix A. In so doing, the reader may see how internal and external tests, including corroborative published sources, can be applied to a specific body of oral historical information.

5

Submerged Forms of Historical Truth

THE TRUTH IN ORALLY COMMUNICATED HISTORY does not always lie in its factual accuracy. Local historians should look for underlying truths contained in values, attitudes, beliefs, and feelings as expressed orally in exaggerations, distortions, and seeming contradictions of historical fact. What people *believe* happened is often as important as what actually happened, for people think, act, and react in accordance with what they believe to be true.

These submerged truths are generally conveyed in narratives, but information about attitudes, as well as facts, may be found in local ballads, songs, and proverbs as well. More often than not, these forms of expression are known and shared only among family or community members. People may not always think of them as communicating historical information and may not sing a ballad or mention a "saying" unless specifically asked to do so. Identifying the hidden truths contained in narratives, ballads, songs, and proverbs not only enriches the local historian's final product, but affords a means of interpreting a significant part of

a community's history through residents' attitudes toward
the past.

Attitudes Toward Past Events

When people talk about the past, they often express frank
opinions about the persons or events they describe. Stories
of atrocities committed by jayhawkers, guerrillas, and
other raiding parties during the period of social and political unrest in the Border States following the Civil War
continue to be told in that part of the country. The accounts
are tinged with disgust, fear, and horror, and the perpetrators of the acts are villified in no uncertain terms.
Likewise, Utah's Mountain Meadows Massacre of 1857,
memorialized in local ballads as well as oral narratives, has
inspired direct expression of feelings about the Mormon
attack on a band of emigrants traveling through Mormon
country. Some oral accounts deplore the action, others
defend it, but none are neutral.

Tense situations may create divisions within a community, with resultant feelings and attitudes. Talk about these
situations often continues unabated for years after the
causative factors have disappeared and culminating events
have taken place. Vivid memories of the Wilder-Davidson
coal miners' strike on Tennessee's Cumberland Plateau in
1932 have spawned a body of oral narratives expressing the
harbored resentment that people in the area feel. Informants in Wilder contend that the greed of those who
bought mineral rights in the area at the turn of the century
set the stage for the bloody labor-management struggle of
the early 1930s. Present residents of the economically
depressed area feel that the broad-form deeds used in early

years deprived local people of their fair share of income from coal deposits on their own land, and that mine management received preferential tax treatment from county and state officials. A lifelong resident of the area commented bitterly, in 1976, "They bought some of the land; they stole some of the land; otherwise, they just took it. We could have had gold doorknobs on our schoolhouses today, with just a fair tax on the coal and lumber that went out of here. But we got nothing."[1]

Sometimes people sit in judgment of an event long after it took place. While any form of oral communication may be used to convey these judgments, perhaps none is more succinct and powerful than the proverb, a short saying in common use that strikingly expresses some obvious truth or familiar experience. A black woman being interviewed in 1961 about the racial war between her people and a group of nearby whites, in southern Kentucky, described a specific episode in which some of the white attackers were killed. She clearly viewed the killings as an act of self-defense against whites who were determined to wipe out the black community, and justified the black response to white aggression by saying, in an emotion-choked voice, "It's a poor frog that won't croak for its own pond."[2] Adages of that kind are charged with human emotion and impart a real feeling for people's sentiments about historical events. While analytical quantification of such statements is not possible, they nonetheless have a place in the historical

1. Coyle Copeland, tape-recorded interview, Crawford, Tennessee, May 15, 1976.

2. Sarah Tooley, tape-recorded interview, Fountain Run, Kentucky, August 20, 1961.

record, for they represent the more human element in history.

Contradictory Attitudes

Because individuals perceive events from their own personal vantage points, the local history researcher is likely to encounter conflicting attitudes toward the same event from different people within the same community, especially when political, social, or moral issues are involved. In the case of the Wilder-Davidson strike, for instance, mine officials viewed the presence of the National Guard as necessary for keeping the peace. The striking miners, on the other hand, saw the guardsmen as "pawns" of management. One of the informants described them disparagingly as "so nervous that they shot at every lightning bug that flew by."[3]

A murder case in Hillsville, Virginia, in 1911 affords a classic example of the way conflicting values and attitudes toward an event within the community can be channeled through local balladry. The story, in brief, is this: Two young men indicted for disturbing the peace fled to avoid arrest. When they were illegally taken into custody, an uncle helped them escape, but turned them over to the law the next day. All three were tried in court, but the uncle refused to accept the guilty verdict. A shoot-out followed in the courtroom and four officials of the law were killed. Three members of the young men's family, including the uncle, were sentenced to be hanged. The lawyers and the judge, aided by newspapers, made the courtroom deaths

3. Coyle Copeland, interview, May 15, 1976.

look like the product of a conspiracy rising out of a long-standing grudge. Other newspaper accounts, particularly those written for northern, urban audiences, represented the shoot-out and resulting deaths in terms of a conflict between uncivilized folk law and the legal processes of orderly government. Two different local ballads about the event reflect these conflicting points of view. One ballad plays down the notion of a family conspiracy and expresses antagonistic feelings toward government. The other criticizes the courtroom "murders" and defends the legal process. Local people who sing one ballad do not sing the other; this fact confirms the polarization of attitudes in the community toward the event and the issues involved.[4] In dealing with contradictory attitudes toward historical events among different factions within the community, it is important to remember that there may not be a right or wrong stance; the researcher who consciously favors one position over the other in writing local history runs the risk of introducing bias into the final product.

Popular Attitudes toward Institutionalized Powers

In talking about the past, people often express fully developed and strikingly consistent attitudes toward social and cultural institutions such as the law, religion, and education. As a case in point, people in northern Fentress County, Tennessee, recount as a major portion of the area's history numerous incidents of violent encounters with law enforcement officials, be they "high sheriffs," revenue

4. Peter R. Aceves, "The Hillsville Tragedy in Court Record, Mass Media and Folk Balladry," *Keystone Folklore Quarterly* 16 (1971): 1–38.

agents, or constables. They also tell of occasions when residents took the law into their own hands, usually with fatal consequences. Viewed as a whole, the Fentress County narratives reveal a consistently negative attitude toward law enforcement; in them, peace officers are portrayed as meddling or intruding, at best, and as cruel and unprincipled, at worst.

A recent occurrence in that same area of Tennessee clearly reveals the way in which attitudes toward institutions, as expressed through orally communicated descriptions of past happenings, color a community's perception of contemporary events. When Billy Dean Anderson, listed among the FBI's ten most wanted criminals, was shot and killed at Pall Mall by FBI agents and local authorities in the summer of 1979, the circumstances of his death—a young man, ambushed in his mother's front yard—accorded so well with the area's traditional attitude toward the law that Anderson was transformed, at his "untimely" death, into a folk hero by community residents, and was eulogized as such in the two local newspapers.

Occasionally, attitudes expressed toward a cultural institution in orally communicated history may seem contradictory or inconsistent. For instance, in many rural communities, older residents proudly recount the history of the early schools and reminisce about their own education in one-room schoolhouses. The inference to be drawn is that education is highly valued in the community. Yet, paradoxically, within the same community, higher education may be regarded as a waste of time. The ultimate value being expressed here about education as an institution is that the three R's as taught and learned in the local grade school provided all the education needed for practical day-by-day living.

Outlaws, who appear to be antiheroes, on the surface, are often glorified in oral descriptions of their nefarious activities. While stories about such figures as Jesse James and Butch Cassidy may not necessarily be historically accurate, their telling allows their narrators to gain vicarious victory over cold, impersonal institutions, such as banks and railroads, that stand always ready to exploit them. In a way, accounts of the deeds of outlaws and outcasts represent a kind of wish fulfillment. Looking for the attitudes behind heroization helps to explain why D. B. Cooper, who parachuted out of an airplane somewhere over the state of Washington, with $50,000 in hijacked cash, and has never been captured, has become a folk hero in the Pacific Northwest.

Values and Beliefs in
Nonfactual or Unverifiable Accounts

Traditional tales and motifs can often masquerade as actual occurrences in a local setting. Yet, their traditionality should not automatically exclude them from further consideration by the local historian, for people would not continue to tell such stories if they did not convey some kind of truth. While that truth may not be historically factual, it may reveal a good deal about a community's system of attitudes, values, and beliefs. The following story, for instance, about a trial in a Western town in 1930, clearly expresses the community's attitudes toward the law:

I remember in 1930 when one of the drunks by the name of Jim Egan pulled a knife on somebody over at one of the Silver Lake dances. They arrested him, and they had him show up for trial, and they had a jury selected from the town here. And if they'd found him guilty, I suppose they would have sent him to jail. Course, everything in the whole trial and whatnot would have been considered illegal, now, in the selection of the jury, but I guess it would have stuck, in those days.

But the dances were pretty rough, and they decided that pulling a knife on somebody was reasonably normal behavior for a Silver Lake dance, and so they acquitted him.[5]

A more humorous example obliquely expresses a negative attitude toward unmarried mothers:

A girl suspected of being pregnant out of wedlock left for another state "for a few months." She soon wrote home that she had met a nice man, fallen in love, and married him. Two weeks later, she again wrote home, this time to announce his illness. A third letter followed almost immediately bearing the sad tidings that her husband had died. Upon receipt of this last piece of news, her Aunt Pinky—known in the community for stating openly what others were thinking silently—said scorchingly, "Well! I knew he would die the minute I heard he was sick!"[6]

Community values are frequently embodied in accounts of the hardships faced by the first immigrants. The stories told about the difficulties people overcame in making a living under the adverse conditions of not knowing the language or the economic system in their new home, for example, express the value placed on adaptability and resourcefulness in these trying situations. In another vein,

5. Forest Stratton, tape-recorded interview, Silver Lake, Oregon, July 8, 1978.
6. Letter from contributor who wishes to remain anonymous, Fort Lauderdale, Florida, March 2, 1980.

family stories can also reveal values and aspirations. One family in Texas, for instance, tells how the family treasure was buried to preserve it from marauding Union soldiers. Historically, of course, the story is specious, for the Union Army never operated in Texas. Yet it serves two real functions: first, it links the family with the pivotal event in American history, the Civil War; and second, it explains the absence of family jewels, whose hiding place had regrettably been forgotten.

People's pride in their home community may be expressed in stories directly or indirectly extolling its virtues. For instance, the place name *Egypt,* which occurs in various communities throughout the United States, commonly has the following legend associated with it: The region or community acquired the designation *Egypt* when it was able to supply surrounding areas with grain, following a crop failure or disaster. The legend thus alludes to the biblical story of Joseph's visit to Egypt during the famine in Israel. Since this particular place-name legend is found in more than one community, the story is not likely to be true in all cases. Yet, in telling the story about their own communities, people express a sense of pride in their region's fertility and desirability.[7]

Sometimes a community's identity hinges on residents' belief in the deeds, real or presumed, of a famous native son or daughter. Godiva of Coventry, England, apotheosized for her famous act of political protest, represents people's propensity to defend some narratives with fanatical en-

---

7. Herbert Halpert, " 'Egypt'—A Wandering Place-Name Legend," in *Buying the Wind: Regional Folklore in the United States,* by Richard M. Dorson (Chicago: University of Chicago Press, 1964), pp. 295–299.

thusiasm, should anyone dare suggest that they have no foundation in historical fact. When it was pointed out to the people of Coventry in 1967 that there was reason to doubt the truth of Lady Godiva's famous ride, the residents were outraged. In London, *The Times* warned historians that "modern citizens have no patience with conflicting theories that surround Godiva's ride," and quoted a statement from a teen-aged girl in Coventry: "What if they find Godiva did not ride at all? Coventry would not be the same. If she had not made the place famous, we would not be here today."[8]

Key Events as Focal Points in Local History

We should be prepared to acknowledge that the view of the past expressed in orally communicated history may conflict with that found in the formal records on which historians typically rely. As a case in point, oral testimonies recorded from villagers between Kabul and Jalalabad, Afghanistan, recount, on a day-to-day basis, the British army's retreat between the two points in 1842. These traditional Afghan recollections conflict with the official version contained in published British accounts in their emphasis on Afghan heroes, their bravery, and their reasons for fighting.[9] Formal historians researching the retreat have ignored the oral traditional narratives surrounding the event—and have failed to make allowances for biased British documents compiled during an era of

8. Quoted by H. R. Ellis Davidson, "Folklore and History," *Folklore* 85 (1974): 75.

9. Louis Dupree, "The Retreat of the British Army from Kabul to Jalalabad in 1842: Folklore and History," *Journal of the Folklore Institute* 4 (1967):50–74.

colonial expansion.[10] This particular example illustrates that the relative emphasis placed by informants on events in local history may not match a formal historian's description of the same events.

When people talk about local history, they are likely to emphasize those events that they consciously or unconsciously feel were most significant in the past. As a result, the "shape" of the past in residents' minds may not be the same as that contained in formal history. For instance, residents of Calumet, Michigan, repeatedly point to the "1913 disaster" as marking the turning point in their community's history. A Christmas party in a Calumet community hall ended in the deaths of seventy people, when a false alarm of fire was called out. Community residents lay the blame for the tragedy on a bitter struggle between the miners' union and mine management and see the beginning of Calumet's economic decline as stemming from that incident, even though the community actually enjoyed a degree of prosperity in later years.[11]

Orally communicated history in Silver Lake, Oregon, offers another example of the way a key event becomes, in residents' minds, the pivotal point for their community's history. In talking about the past, residents focus on the homesteading that took place in the area during the first two decades of the twentieth century, although several other events preserved in written accounts of the area—including a disastrous fire on Christmas Eve, 1894, and a bloody range war in 1905—seem equally worthy of atten-

10. Kenneth C. Wylie, "The Uses and Misuses of Ethnohistory," *Journal of Interdisciplinary History* 3 (1973): 719.

11. William Ivey, " ' The 1913 Disaster': Michigan Local Legend," *Folklore Forum* 3 (1970): 100–114.

tion. The preoccupation with homesteading as the primary topic of orally communicated history in Silver Lake is even more striking in view of the fact that the homesteading effort ultimately failed, and most of the thousands of people who had moved to the area between 1909 and 1916 were gone by 1920. One explanation for the emphasis on the homesteading period is that residents unconsciously use the failure of the homesteaders to account for Silver Lake's present underdeveloped state.[12] By paying attention to topics brought up over and over again by informants, either in informal conversations or in formal interviews, the local historian may be able to identify residents' perspectives on the course of local history, by noting which events receive lavish attention and which ones get short shrift, and by remembering that orally communicated history is always retrospective: the past is perceived through the screen of the present.

12. For a fuller discussion, see Barbara Allen, "Talking about the Past: A Folkloristic Study of Orally Communicated History" (Ph.D. diss., University of California at Los Angeles, 1980).

6

Producing a Manuscript from Oral Sources

THIS MANUAL DESCRIBES AND DISCUSSES THE KINDS of historical information available from oral sources. What remains to be done is to indicate how that orally communicated information can be integrated into a written historical narrative. Specific procedures involved in collecting oral information in local history research, such as preliminary library research, setting up and conducting interviews, indexing and transcribing tapes, and archiving the tapes and the typewritten transcriptions for subsequent use fall outside the scope of this book. There are a number of handbooks, however, that provide this basic information, including Willa K. Baum's *Oral History for the Local Historical Society*, second edition (1971) and her *Transcribing and Editing Oral History* (1977), both published by the American Association for State and Local History; Cullom Davis et al., *Oral History: From Tape to Type* (Chicago: American Library Association, 1977); Edward D. Ives, *The Tape-Recorded Interview: A Manual for Field Workers in Folklore and Oral History* (Knoxville: University of Tennessee Press, 1980); William W. Moss, *Oral History Program Manual* (New York: Praeger, 1974); and Gary L. Shumway and William G. Hartley, *An Oral History Primer* (Fullerton, Cal.: California State University, 1973). All of these manuals address, among other topics, the pre-interview process, the interview, legal considerations, and guides for transcribing and editing tapes.

In researching written materials prior to recording oral information, for example, the local historian should look at newspaper files, legal records, books, and various other promising sources. Information gained in this manner will serve to direct attention to topics of potential interest, as well as to provide valuable background information. Preliminary inquiries and investigation may also help the researcher to steer away from asking for information about topics already well-documented in print. Replication of what is already known is time-consuming and usually nonproductive, but one may occasionally wish to gather oral information about well-documented facets of history, to gain a personal, human perspective on the written record. Conducting preliminary research means surveying oral as well as written sources of information. Procedures such as listening to and participating in informal conversations or placing queries in local newspapers can aid the researcher in locating and selecting informants who are most knowledgeable about the topic at hand.

At the outset of each interview, the researcher will need to explain the research project to the informant and obtain his or her signature on a release form that indicates the informant's consent to the interviewer's intended use of the materials. Specific information about legal release forms is available in most of the manuals listed at the beginning of this chapter. Information about U.S. copyright law can be obtained from the *General Guide to the Copyright Act of 1976* (Washington, D.C.: U.S. Government Printing Office, 1977). If information from an informal, unrecorded conversation is to be used in a written manuscript, legal permission from its source must, of course, also be secured.

Once the interview is completed, the researcher should prepare a typed transcript of the tape, or type up the interview notes, if the conversation was not recorded. (Whether to transcribe the entire tape or not depends largely on the dictates of individual research projects.) Oral historians disagree among themselves about the ways in which transcribing should be done. Some insist that the transcript should be an absolutely accurate representation of the tape; at the other extreme are those who argue that the transcription should be edited into a smooth narrative in polished English. Our recommendation is to transcribe tapes verbatim, then edit the transcription to remove false starts, *uhs, ahs,* and stutterings, and "crutch" words and phrases such as "well," and "you know." Spelling and word forms should be standardized—*get,* not *git; heard,* not *heerd; going,* not *goin'*—but texts should not be altered to the extent of correcting grammar. If the informant said, "I seen," the text should not be changed to read "I saw."[1]

1. There are two schools of thought about reproducing the sounds of regional speech. One group cogently argues that television is rapidly standardizing regional speech and that, without taking care to reproduce the authentic sounds of regional accents, such speech may be irretrievable within a few years. Our feeling about the matter is that, since the sounds are recorded on tape, attempts to reproduce speech sounds in print are not necessary (as long as the original tape is preserved); furthermore, such attempts can be distracting to the reader and demeaning to the original speakers.

103

After formal records have been reviewed and after orally communicated information has been obtained through interviews and conversations, the researcher should prepare an outline of the manuscript to be written. If the manuscript is to rely heavily on written sources of information, oral materials will be complementary, in the main. On the other hand, if the topic is one about which little has been written previously, oral sources will serve as the primary documents. In either case, the general procedures for incorporating them into a written narrative are the same.

Organizing Oral Materials by Topic

The local historian should make copies of all transcriptions and all notes. The originals should be retained in a master file; the copies can then be cut up and placed in vertical file folders according to the various subject categories that will form the chapters or divisions of the manuscript.

Once the major categories have been established, one should go through each vertical folder and further divide the contents into subcategories to be addressed in the chapter. Again, it may be necessary to use scissors to divide transcriptions of the oral texts by topic. Be sure that each cutting is labeled properly and carries the name of the informant and the date of the interview or conversation. For a section dealing with settlement, for example, possible subdivisions could be "The Era of the Indian," "Exploration," "The Coming of White Settlers," "Homes and Early Life Styles," "Early Political Institutions," "Religion on the Frontier," and so on.

Integrating Oral Texts into the Written Narrative

Oral sources slated for use as complementary to or supportive of printed sources should be woven into the over-all historical account written by the local historian. By no means should the oral materials be lumped together into a separate chapter and labeled "folklore." Much of what is passed along orally is deeply grounded in fact, so that the local historian can quite properly include such oral materials as historical legends and anecdotes throughout the manuscript to complement and illuminate the formal record. For instance, a discussion of the manner in which the community was settled is the place to include place-name legends. It should be clearly indicated that these explanatory legends were derived from oral tradition and that the writer makes no claim for their historical accuracy, not even for the "logical" ones, unless every step has been taken to prove their veracity. In like manner, oral reports of pioneer encounters with Indians, wild animals, and the vicissitudes of the environment may also fit well into this part of the manuscript. Even apocryphal stories of this type help to illuminate the nature of the harsh and frightening experiences encountered by pioneers in newly-occupied areas.

Disasters, in the form of tornadoes, fire, floods, train wrecks, labor disputes, and the like, are likely to be part of the history of any community or group. By using oral accounts to complement written records, the local historian has an excellent opportunity to reveal how both natural and human-induced disasters affected life for the individual as well as for the community as a whole. Old newspaper accounts may provide the bare facts surrounding the calamities, but nothing can take the place of eyewitness accounts or personal narratives.

Summarizing. Oral accounts may be incorporated in summary form into the local historian's written manuscript, or they may be included verbatim. We suggest that the oral text be summarized before inclusion if it is rambling and disjointed. The following example, drawn from oral tradition in the Arkansas Ozarks, illustrates the need to summarize the text before incorporating it into the written manuscript. This is the unedited transcript:

> I think that, that I know, that later on somebody there maybe did find that money there; all of it, or maybe part of it. I don't know if they found all of it or not, or anything at all. But later on—sometime after that—why, back south of where he lived, about—oh, it wasn't a quarter of a mile, but it was better than a quarter of it, half a quarter of a mile—why, there was a house on the side of the road. I don't think anybody was living in it at this time. But one night there was a—somebody come there and dug a great big old deep hole in the ground—a hole as deep as a grave—and pulled out a pot. Don't know what was in it, if there was gold, or anything like that, such as gold—or anything about that. But the print of the bottom of the pot, and the three legs, why, that—that pot set on, was in the bottom of the hole that they dug, just as plain as anything.[2]

The summary of the text follows. Note that no relevant details have been omitted:

> An undetermined amount of buried money, perhaps gold, may have been dug up less than one-quarter mile south of a

2. Name withheld to avoid possible embarrassment on the part of the informant.

house thought to be deserted. One night, an unknown party removed a three-legged pot from a hole in the ground described by the informant as being "as deep as a grave." Imprints in the ground, made by the pot's bottom and three legs, were seen by others.

Using Verbatim Texts. When oral texts are coherent and articulate, they may be used in their entirety, framed on both sides with the writer's own words. Handling texts in such a manner allows the informants to speak for themselves and in their own words. As a result, there is less danger of misinterpreting the speakers' meaning, and the printed page is richer for the inclusion of the human voice in the historical record. The following example illustrates a suggested narrative framing device for utilizing oral texts in their entirety:

With guns and ammunition ready, the defenders went down the lane a few feet from the house and hid behind a row of low shrubs. Tom Jones, their leader, recalled in an interview his instructions to the group and described the initial part of the attack:

" 'When the last one of them gets up here even with me, I'll fire the first shot.' So I fired the first shot, and the others opened up and let their guns really talk. The invaders started shooting, but they were so shot up and scared that all but about eight ran off. Some ran into grapevines and barbed wire and marked up their necks and faces with scars that they took with them to the grave."

Sally Anderson, whose husband was among the six defenders, reiterated the part about the invaders who were injured as they fled:

"I know there was one man that got hurt in the throat. He'd speak, or try to; claimed to be sick. But they said he got stuck in the throat and it ruined his speech. He was unable to ever talk right again."

Jim Booker, now deceased, was among those who broke and ran when the shooting started. In the words of Paul Thomas, who recalled hearing Booker talk about the infamous event:
"Jim said a couple of the younger defenders chased him down into the woods. He ducked into a big old hollow log.
"The chasers came on down there and hopped up on this log that Jim was in. He said he was really scared—afraid that they'd hear his heart pounding against the log.
"But they didn't find him. They figured he'd got away, you know. Jim said, 'When I got out of that scrape, I didn't go back any more.' "

In instances where full texts are unavailable or inappropriate, insert quotations or portions of quotations from recorded material as often as possible, to allow the narrators' insights, personalities, and philosophies to dominate the written account. Consider for example:

People of both ethnic groups remembered the proprietor of the store as a person who would never "sell bad merchandise," nor cheat even when the customer "could not read the weight on the scales." One informant, who prefers to remain anonymous, eulogized the proprietor as a person who would "cheat herself before she would a customer." "If you ask me," the informant continued, "there was never a better woman in the community."[3]

At this point, the local historian/writer may elect to complete the story, with or without use of additional quotes and texts obtained from oral sources, by drawing upon newspaper descriptions, court records, and other published sources. For instance, it would be totally appropriate to use an oral text to conclude the discussion about the

3. All of the above examples are hypothetical.

proprietor, especially if someone contributed an especially insightful story about this outstanding businesswoman. Note that the quotations in the foregoing examples are clearly shown to be obtained from oral sources. That differentiation should always be made when oral and printed sources are both drawn upon to explicate an event. Readers should not have to wonder about the nature of the source.

Presenting Conflicting Views

In the event of conflicting oral testimonies, be careful to identify the authors of each viewpoint. Do not make sweeping general statements, such as "Most informants felt that . . . ," or "A few persons claimed. . ." Be specific; all informants are entitled to a say in the matter. By identifying the speakers, the local historian cannot be accused of bias in the choice of words used to document one position or another. If two persons oppose five others on a certain point, say so. If all seven contend for different positions, all seven may be worth quoting in the manuscript. The following example illustrates that point:

In describing the disastrous Christmas Eve fire in Silver Lake, Oregon, Genny Boatwright stated that

> "It took a day and a half for the doctor to get here from Lakeview [one hundred miles to the south]." Neva Warner, however, whose father lost his first wife in the fire, claimed that the trip took three days, because "there was a heavy snow on the ground." In his book, Reub Long corroborated what Mrs. Boatwright had said, pinpointing the doctor's arrival at six o'clock on the morning of December 26, thirty-six hours after the fire. Mr. Long also named the man who had made the heroic ride as Ed O'Farrell. A newspaper article based on an interview with another old-timer, Kob Buick,

disagreed on this point, however. "Ira Bradley was the one who fetched Dr. Daly," Buick insisted.[4]

While the details in accounts like these are fluid, the core of truth remains; someone rode for the doctor, and he covered the distance quickly. The oral improvisation on minor details of historical events, in fact, seems to help keep those events firmly fixed in people's memories and ensures their continuance in orally communicated history.

Indicating Corroborative Sources

The historian using orally communicated history should cite formal records, when possible, to verify or dispute a claim made by orally communicated history. This is normally done by providing footnotes. If the main written account, based on oral recollections, claims that a certain planter owned fifteen slaves at the outbreak of the Civil War, the documenting footnote might cite the Slave Census for 1860 as listing only six slaves for the planter in question, thus indicating that the oral account is at variance on that point. Or, if one informant claims that an event took place in 1901, since it happened on his seventh birthday and he remembers it for that reason, the researcher may wish to indicate in a footnote that a newspaper account verified the event as taking place exactly when claimed.

---

4. Genny Boatwright, tape-recorded interview, Fort Rock, Oregon, July 4, 1978; Neva Warner, tape-recorded interview, Silver Lake, Oregon, July 6, 1978; Reuben Long and E. R. Jackman, *The Oregon Desert* (Caldwell, Ida.: Caxton Printers, 1964), pp. 126–127; "Buick Says Bradley Rode to Get Dr. Daly in 1894," *Lake County Examiner*, November 27, 1969, p. 3.

Use of Fictitious Names

The historian's main concern in local historical research should not be with sensational matters pertaining to the personal lives of the subjects interviewed, when such information has little or nothing to do with the centrality of the research being done. On the other hand, when these personal aspects are deemed essential to the fully explicated historical record, they should not be glossed over. When it is necessary to use information of a highly personal or previously confidential nature, it is wise—and sometimes necessary—to change the names of the personalities identified in the oral accounts as a means of avoiding unnecessary embarrassment to the persons mentioned. Substituting a pseudonym may persuade the narrator not to place restrictions on the use of the interview material; it may also prevent litigation.[5] In the event of name changes, indicate in a footnote that pseudonyms have replaced the real names in both your own written description and in the oral accounts provided by informants, so as to retain continuity in the finished manuscript. People in the community will probably still know who the chief actors are, even when names have been changed, but the researcher is less likely to be accused of defamation of name or character.

Subjective Comments in Footnotes

In writing the manuscript, the researcher should not intrude subjective feelings about a topic into the written

---

5. Nothing from oral sources should be published that would implicate informants in a crime or create hazards for them professionally, personally, or legally.

narrative itself. If it seems necessary to enter an argument or contradict a statement, do so in a footnote. To enter one's own subjective reactions in the text would be to bias the account.

Mechanical Details

Footnoting oral sources. As in the case of written materials quoted or cited in footnotes, credit should be given to informants who contribute items of orally communicated history. Arabic numerals calling attention to these oral contributions may be inserted within a sentence, at the end of a sentence, or at the end of a paragraph. The only difference between citing oral sources and formal sources is the structure and content of the footnote itself. Thus, when an oral source is cited for the first time in the manuscript, identify the nature of the interview (that is, whether done with tape recorder or with pencil and pad), the name of the informant, place of residence, and the date of the interview. In subsequent footnotes which refer to this specific interview, only the name of the informant and the date of the interview need be included. The date is especially helpful in preventing confusion when more than one interview or conversation was conducted with the informant. The following are examples of footnotes in which oral sources are cited for the first time.

1. Sarah Anne Farley, tape-recorded interview, Boise, Idaho, August 30, 1979.

1. Sarah Anne Farley, formal interview using pen and notebook, Boise, Idaho, August 31, 1979.

1. Sarah Anne Farley, informal conversation, Boise, Idaho, September 12, 1979.

MANUSCRIPTS FROM ORAL SOURCES

1. Sarah Anne Farley, telephone conversation, Boise, Idaho, November 3, 1979.

As stated above, the informant's name and the date of the interview will serve in subsequent citations.

In the event that oral materials were obtained from tapes or manuscripts on deposit in a library or archive, the footnotes should give the name of the informant, location of the archive, tape or manuscript number, year of the interview, and manuscript page number, as shown below:

1. Samuel Smith, Archive of Folklore, Folklife, and Oral History, Western Kentucky University, Bowling Green, Kentucky. T-781-1971.

1. Samuel Smith, unpublished manuscript, Archive of Folklore, Folklife, and Oral History, Bowling Green, Kentucky, Western Kentucky University. M-903-1973-13.

Bibliography entries. An alphabetical listing of the persons who contributed the orally communicated history used in the manuscript should be included in the bibliography. A minimum bibliographic entry for informants should include at least the contributor's name, place of residence, sex, date of birth, place of birth, major occupations engaged in across the years, and dates of interviews. Sample bibliographic entry:

> Farley, Sarah Anne, Boise, Idaho; female, b. 1 February 1899, Missoula, Montana; housekeeper, newspaper reporter (1917-1933), City Clerk (1943-1951); author of three pamphlets dealing with the history of Boise; interviews on August 30–31, 1979; other conversations on September 12 and November 3, 1979.

Archive collections should also be included in the bibliography. The entry should contain the name of the institution where the archive is located, its geographical location, and the name of the archive or special collection. Sample archive references:

> Bowling Green, Kentucky. Western Kentucky University. Archive of Folklore, Folklife, and Oral History. Tape 781-1971.
>
> Bowling Green, Kentucky. Western Kentucky University. Archive of Folklore, Folklife, and Oral History. Manuscript 903-1973.

A helpful reference on editing historical works in preparation for publication is Richard Cox's "An Annotated Bibliography of Basic Readings on Archives and Manuscripts," published in the September 1980 issue of the American Association for State and Local History's monthly *History News*. For help in handling citations of formal sources of history, refer to a standard writer's manual or style sheet, such as *A Manual for Writers of Term Papers, Theses, and Dissertations*, by Kate Turabian (Chicago: University of Chicago Press, 1973); the *MLA Handbook for Writers of Research Papers, Theses, and Dissertations* (New York: Modern Language Association, 1977); or the University of Chicago Press's own comprehensive *A Manual of Style for Authors, Editors, and Copywriters*, twelfth edition, revised (1969).

Appendix A

The Legend of Calvin Logsdon

The Story

A triple murder, described by the Nashville, Tennessee, *Republican Banner* as "the most fiendish deed of blood ever perpetrated within the borders of Tennessee," occurred November 19, 1868, in Fentress County, Tennessee, north of Jamestown. Clubbed to death with an ax, shovel, and hatchet were Catharine Galloway, forty-six; her daughter Lucy, twenty-seven; and Lucy's son, four. Lucy's eight-year-old son was also beaten and left for dead, while a three-week-old daughter was left unharmed. A neighbor discovered the mutilated bodies a day or so later and reported the matter to officials.

James Calvin Logsdon, nineteen, was captured and jailed, along with two female accomplices who then turned state's evidence on Logsdon and were released. After three trials and three years of confinement in Nashville, Logsdon was sentenced to be hanged.

He was sent back to Jamestown, under heavy guard, to

await his execution. Hundreds of people, including women and children, most of them believing Logsdon to be innocent, witnessed his April 5, 1872, hanging. Because the rope broke twice during the proceedings, Logsdon was actually hanged three times. At the gallows, he predicted an event that did ensue: he said that a three-day deluge of rain, accompanied by flooding, would take place, as a demonstration of his innocence.

Logsdon's story has crystallized into legend told throughout an eight-county area in Tennessee and Kentucky. Nashville newspapers picked up the story, once the Logsdon trial entered the Tennessee Supreme Court, and the trial briefs are extant. Two sets of official kinds of corroborative evidence—court records and newspaper accounts—make it possible to examine the oral traditions surrounding the hanging. Further, the published diary of the Methodist circuit-riding preacher who attended Logsdon during his last hours is also available as corroborative evidence.

The Logsdon legend begins and ends in oral tradition, but oral tradition is silent on the middle portion of the story—the Supreme Court proceedings. The court records address only the details of the crime, and naturally do not mention the hanging and the flood. The newspaper accounts are concerned only with Supreme Court hearings and omit the murders and the hanging. The preacher's diary describes only the death scene. Since it takes all of these sources to piece together the complete story, there is ample opportunity to look at the trustworthiness of the oral traditional record. The texts printed below were transcribed from oral interviews and provide the basis for the following demonstration of the way oral materials can be weighed against written evidence and evaluated for historical accuracy.

Oral Testimonies

The Murders

The following texts deal with the full spectrum of the Logsdon killings and with Logsdon's subsequent execution by hanging.

1. George Patton, Forbus, Tennessee, February 12, 1972 (Interviewed by Linda White)

He first killed three people, you know; that's Logsdon I'm talking about. Two women and a boy, and he left.

They tracked him up there . . . by Chanute and on through by Albany. And he told them when he got down there, "Did y'all hear about that [family] that got killed up in Tennessee yesterday, up in Fentress County?" And so they knowed that he had to know something about it, or it wasn't so, one [or the other]. And so they kinda watched him, and put a man on a good horse. So he got on him and came over here [to Fentress County] and found out he [Logsdon] was the man. And they just brought him over here, you know, and they kept him in that jail down there [in Nashville] three years.

They first tried him in Overton County down at Livingston, and he proved he was in Scott County, that it wasn't there. Well, they tried him in Scott County and that's twice he's tried and in two different counties. And they proved it was in Fentress County; that was three times

117

he was tried. And when they brought him up here [to Fentress County], they actually proved he did do the killing at what we used to call Possum Trot. I can show you where the old house logs is, now, where the house stood. I've seen the house standing there.

When they done that, they brought him right here [Jamestown] and they hung him. They started out down through there [to the gallows] and, of course . . . they wasn't nothing then but horses and horseback riders. And they began to sing a song right along behind him, and they couldn't sing it, not a one of them. He knowed the song— and they'd go to crying; they couldn't sing it. He told them, let him sing it; and he sung right on down there [to the gallows]. My daddy saw him hung. Before they hung him, he got up there, sitting on his coffin, just a-singing as good as anybody can; in tune; never broke down a bit. My dad said he [Logsdon] never did break down until the second time they hung him. The first time (they said he had a awful big neck, and he was a big heavy man), and they said he held himself. See, he had his hands tied behind him, you know, couldn't get no hold of the rope, and they hung him, and he was so big and heavy, the rope broke. [The Sheriff] jumped up there and tied it [the noose] with a rope now, you know, and that made it a little shorter every time, but he put him up there again, and directly he fell again, and when he fell again, he broke it again. And my daddy said that when he fell that time, that the blood just gushed out of his mouth. . . . He said, "If you gonna kill me, kill me; if you don't, turn me loose." And [the hangman] he sorta [was] like Logsdon, he sorta bloodthirsty hisself; he just jerked him back up there and tied it together. It was a short,

just a short piece now, and whenever they hanged him, he
said it never broke his neck.

2. Mrs. C. E. Toney, Allardt, Tennessee, March 18, 1978

Years after that, my mother's father married this girl they
said was the one that killed these people.

These two girls turned state's evidence—Jane and Eliza
Brown—against Logsdon in the trial. They hung him in
place of the girls; they come free, see.

I'm not sure, but I think Jane was a-courting Cal Logsdon.

Lucy and her mother lived there together. . . . This girl
[Lucy] was out of wedlock when she had these children.

Jane's father [Mr. Brown] was going to marry this girl
[Lucy Galloway]. But Jane wasn't going to let him take that
girl. They didn't believe in that.

So they [Cal and the Brown sisters] went on Saturday
night. And the old lady [Catharine Galloway] was carding
wool here in the corner by her fireplace in the lamplight.
Jane, and Eliza, her sister, and Cal Logsdon went in for the
purpose of killing this girl. They killed her and went around
to the old mother, and she said, "I never harmed you folks
in my life." She said, "Don't hit me." And they killed her
with a shovel. And so years after that, my mother's father
(from Calfkiller Creek) . . . name of James Short, married
this Jane. They say Cal Logsdon killed them, but my
mother always said Jane did it. . . . The family feels like
Jane did the killing.

Jane Brown Short raised my mother. The reason Mother
always said Jane did the killing was this: my grandfather
was what you called a rich man, then. He had a big farm and
all kinds of stock. And all these stock buyers would come to

my grandfather Short's . . . and stay all night, buying stock and talking stock trade. Well, Mother said that, any time that Jane got out of the house, on a real dark night, somebody would raise up in front of her, she said—two of them. And she [Jane] could see them. She said, "Why, I could put my hand on their head."

And Mother said, "Now, Jane, you don't see no such as that."

She said, "All right"; she said, "I want you to go out with me tonight, and I'll show them to you!"

Well, Mother said they went out between the house and the barn that night. And it was just black; you couldn't see a thing. And she said Jane said, "Now, there they are." (My mother's name was Amanda, and they called her Mandy.) Said, "Mandy, don't you see them there?"

Mother said, "I couldn't see a thing in the world." She said, "No, Jane, and you don't see them!"

"Yes!" she said, "I do!" She said, "I could lay my hand on their head, if they had a head, but they don't have a head."

And she saw that all her life!! Till she died!

She thought they was the two she had killed.

My mother told her a many a time, "Jane, you just as sure killed them two women as you're standing here."

"Aw," she'd say, "you little fool, I didn't do it." She'd deny it, but Mother said she did. Mother said the reason she knew she did that, "she was the hardest-hearted person I ever saw in my life." She said "If she got mad at a child . . . she'd hate that child as long as she lived."

She said Cal Logsdon was a clear man. Then when Uncle Joe Taylor (that was Mr. Ward's, my husband's, uncle) went to hang Cal, and the rope broke, Uncle Joe always said, "That man wasn't guilty, or the rope wouldn't have broke."

120

And it broke twice. There were two witnesses against Cal. And all they [the jury] could do was to take the best evidence in court. Jane and Eliza were actually tried, but they come clear, on account of being the two against Cal. And my mother always said that this hard-hearted Jane was what got him into it. She just said, "Now, Cal, listen." (They lived close together.) "My father is going to marry that notorious thing, and you're going with us and we're going to kill her."

That little boy, you know, when they put him on the witness stand, was eight years old. This Mr. Brown went to see this girl. (They was to get married just shortly after this happened—a week or two weeks.) He went on Sunday morning to see this girl that he was going to marry. Said the little boy's hair was sticking out through the crack under the door. And the old man thought he'd got up while the others were getting breakfast and laid down there and went to sleep. He retch down here and pulled the little fellow's hair, but he never moved. Pulled his hair two or three times; still didn't move. Then he thought something was wrong. He went in, and there they were, dead.

It rained at the hanging, but they wasn't no flood. . . . They said Cal Logsdon was from a good family. They said he was a nice boy, from a good family.

3. Letter based on oral information from Mrs. Ona Barton to Lynwood Montell, January 10, 1978

. . . I have talked with a Mr. Earl Taylor of Jamestown. The sheriff, J. C. Taylor, that did the hanging, was a brother of Earl Taylor's grandfather. . . . Mr. Earl told me that he had heard his folk talk about Logston, that the sheriff had said before he would perform another hanging he would resign from being a sheriff.

I have found that Logston's mother's name was Margaret Logston, and I think the Galloway women's names were Lucy and Catharine, but the child's name I do not know. I did not remember to tell you when you were here last week, but I found out that Logston was courting one of the Evans women that were connected with the murders. My sister-in-law told me that she had heard her mother tell that they were.

Sincerely

/s/ Ona Barton

The following texts describe the murders only.

4. Lonnie Barton, Daily Crouch, Fred Johnson, Forbus, Tennessee, November 16, 1977

Crouch: Logston killed two women and a child. There was another youngster he thought he had killed, but he later revived, and he told the story. They were Galloways.

Johnson: I always heard the women were sisters.

Crouch: The house where they were killed was a log house.

Johnson: How come that child to live, back then they had featherbeds, and that child was buried in a featherbed. It was cold, snowy weather. It was just sunk down in it—a warm place.

Crouch: The weapon used was an axe. The motive was robbery. I reckon it was a robbery he was doing. Fred's daddy there kept a scrapbook. He said what tripped [Logston] up, he went on, and he was crossing the Cumberland River on a ferry; he asked the ferryman if he'd heard of this killing over here. Otherwise, he would have gone scot free, because there was no witnesses, except that little boy.

Johnson: See, the bodies hadn't been found at that time when he asked that [on the ferry]; nobody knew it.

Crouch: Now, that seems to be the general deduction.

Montell: Who were the two women implicated in the Galloway murder?

Johnson: That's the two women that he was staying with. I understood that he was staying with them women.

Crouch: This testimony of the ferryman clinched the whole deal.

Johnson: That was at Burkesville, over there crossing the Cumberland.

Crouch: He was leaving the country; going up into Kentucky, I imagine. I expect that was the most evidence against him. That and the child's testimony. It was an eight-year-old child. He was more stunned than seriously hurt.

Barton: I think it was three days before they ever found the child; that's the way I always heard it.

5. Dennis Crockett, Mrs. Flossie Crockett, J. D. Lowrey, Edd Moody, Moodyville, Tennessee, November 16, 1977

Lowrey:	The people's name that was killed was Evans; there were two women and a boy, but the boy survived. He crossed the Cumberland River at Rowena Ferry, and he told the ferryman that somebody had killed the Evans women that night, and the neighbors didn't know about it at that time.
F. Crockett:	I've heard my great-grandma tell about it. And she said how come these women were killed, and Logston said he wasn't to blame, that he wasn't really the guilty person, because they's women jealous of the Evans women.
Moody:	They thought their father was going to marry one of them.
Lowrey:	They thought their father was going to marry one of them, so they [daughters] gave him forty dollars to kill them.
D. Crockett:	I know who they accused of being there— I've heard them say. It was Hert Hill's wife, whoever she was. Who was she?
Moody:	She was an Evans.
D. Crockett:	I've always heard that; I don't know if it's true or not. I've always heard that talked, way back. . . . They said the little boy identified him; they would line him up with other men, and then they'd take him [Logsdon] and re-dress him, put different clothes on him, but said the little boy picked

	him out every time. Now, he thought he had killed the little boy. Said he crawled up in the fireplace.
Montell:	How did he kill these people?
Moody:	With a hatchet!
Lowrey:	That's my understanding, too.
Moody:	He hit him [the Galloway boy] in the head with a hatchet, but it didn't kill him. He thought he had.
Montell:	How many were killed?
Moody:	Two women, and the boy was injured. . . .
D. Crockett:	These women hired him to do this. They thought their father was interested in one of the women and was going to marry her. And they didn't want that. I've heard it said they give him forty dollars to do the killing.
Montell:	How did the boy manage to survive?
Lowrey:	I don't know. They hit him. They had wounded him.
F. Crockett:	He crawled up in the fireplace.
Lowrey:	Crawled up in the fireplace. He thought he had killed him, is the way I understood it, at the time when he left them. But he was in the fireplace and wasn't dead when they found him.

6. Norman Wood, Mrs. Mae Wood, Jamestown, Tennessee, June 18, 1979

N. Wood:	A man come to the door, and the little Galloway boy's hair was sticking under the door there, and he pulled the hair, and no-

body moved. And went in there, then, and then this one boy wasn't dead, and he got him out.

M. Wood: And he identified Logsdon, later, this little child did, [at] some kind of a public gathering.

7. Mrs. Sarah Jane Koger, Mrs. Ona Barton, Jamestown, Tennessee, June 18, 1979

Koger: Well, Logsdon and the Evanses had robbed the John Wright store. And these Galloway ladies was witnesses against them. They was going to have a trial about it, and before they could, before the date of the trial, why, the Galloways was killed. Logsdon and the Evanses, they claimed, was the ones killed them. They was Old Lady Galloway and her daughter. And the daughter had three children. They killed one of the children, the little girl, and they left the baby, and they struck the little boy in the head with an axe. He was laying on the hearth in front of the fire, and they didn't kill him. They thought they had killed him. But the people in the country thought that the hearth, the fire in the hearth, you know, kept him alive. They found these women when the son of a neighbor's went in to see about them, and they found them. This baby, they said, was almost froze to death. It was—been crawling around, you know, on the bed where its mother laid. They carried the Galloway people up to Absalom Wright's home and laid them out there. They carried this little wounded boy up there, and they placed him on a pallet in front of the fire. And one of the Evans women, they said, went around and squatted down by him. Said she said, "Who hurt you, honey?" Said he said, "You should know. You was there." Then this Logsdon, he took it all on hisself, and, of course, the Evans women come out of it. It was Fetny and Mandy Evans, was the way Grandmother told it.

Montell: Why did he take it all on himself?

Koger: Now, tell about your folks moving in the house with Mrs. Wright.

Koger: To clear these women. He was a-dating one of them. She was his girlfriend.

Barton: Now, tell about your folks moving in the house with Mrs. Wright.

Koger: Well, Absalom Wright's wife was the one told it to my grandmother and my mother. It was her home, you know, where they carried them to and laid them out. My grandmother at that time was a-living down here on the Obey River, and she moved up to Wright's and moved in one part of the Wright home.

Montell: Who found the Galloway bodies after they had been murdered?

Koger: They found them in the house where they lived.

Montell: Who were "they"?

127

Koger: . . . a son of the neighbors.

Montell: And how long after they were killed?

Koger: Well, I guess maybe the next day. I don't know. They didn't tell. But it was pretty close from the time they was killed, by that baby, you know, still being alive. It couldn't have lasted very long, and it [being so] cold. They said the biggest snow was on the ground; it was [an] awful bad time. . . .

They said he was six, seven years old. And he was a witness against them, you know; he knowed them all; they'd been to his home before, they said. They was all well acquainted, and the child recognized them, you know. Grandma said that Mrs. Wright said she had seen the old lady different times, since she was killed, which I don't believe it. I don't believe in ghosts. But said she [Mrs. Wright] was sitting out on the front porch one night and said the moon was shining real bright. And she seen a woman coming up the road and she thought it was a neighbor, and she was fixing to say "Bah" at her, you know, just to kind of scare [her]. Said the moon shined on her comb. (She had a big high-top comb, kindly—it was like a Spanish comb, you know. They've got great high tops to them.) And said when she turned her head, said the moon shined on that comb, and she knowed it was the comb that Mrs. Galloway always wore in her hair. Said Mrs. Wright said she had seen her dif-

	ferent times; but said that was the plainest that she ever seen her.
Montell:	Why would Mrs. Galloway's ghost be there at *this* house?
Koger:	Well, maybe because they carried her up there and laid her out, when she didn't want to be!
Montell:	Now, there's one more question I want to ask about because I can't resolve it. The court records say that it was Eliza and Jane Brown who . . .
Koger:	Well, I never did hear them called Brown . . . until me and Ona'd been talking about it, and she said she'd heard them called Browns. But now I'll tell you what, I knowed a brother of these girls; I knowed him and knowed his family well, and they was Evanses. John ("Wobbler") Evans. His name was John, and they gave him the nickname of "Wobbler." Called him *John Wobbler Evans.* And I knowed his children well.
Montell:	And now, name his two sisters again, who helped rob the store.
Koger:	Well, Fetny was one, and Mandy was the other.

8. Byrd Bryant, Eastland, Tennessee, October 17, 1979 (Interviewed by Rita Bryan and Kevin Hunter)

Hunter:	Did she ever tell you how she came to escape being murdered?

Bryant:	No, because she didn't know. She's just a little tiny baby, laying in bed.
Bryan:	Did they find here in the bed covered up or something?
Bryant:	Yeah, they found her in bed. And him [uncle] on the floor.
Hunter:	Who did you hear this from?
Bryant:	I heard her tell it.
Hunter:	She told you this? Did she ever tell you who she thought did the killings?
Bryant:	A fellow name of Logsdon.
Hunter:	Did anybody help him do this?
Bryant:	Two women. I don't know the women.
Hunter:	Can you tell us about your Uncle James? You said he was beaten up real bad, and they thought he was dead.
Bryant:	Oh, yeah; they tramped his fingers. I've heard her [tell that], to see if he was dead. And he didn't move. And so they went on and left him. And Mother, she was just a tine-sy baby, you know, laying in bed. And they had to put a silver dollar in top his head, up here, where they hit him in the head with an axe, busted his skull.

9. Sam Bryant, Eastland, Tennessee, October 17, 1979 (Interviewed by Rita Bryan and Kevin Hunter)

Bryant:	My mother's name was Mary Jane, Mary Jane Galloway. And Uncle James was knocked in the head. They killed her oldest brother. I think they said he was about eight years old. They run him outdoors and run

130

him around the house and caught him after they had done killed my grandmother and great-grandmother. They brought him back into the house, and they killed him. [At another point in the interview, Mr. Bryant stated that the two Brown sisters took the boy to Logsdon, who did the actual killing of the boy.] So there was three of them killed. And they thought they had Uncle James killed, when they knocked him in the head. But he came to, you know, after they found him. My mother was three weeks old; she laid in the bed all night. She was in the bed, covered up, and they didn't see her.

Bryan: Who discovered the bodies?

Bryant: It was somebody that lived there; a neighbor, close to them. And he come by, the next morning. There was a big snow on the ground, and the door was open about so wide [three to five inches]. And said this boy's hair was sticking out the edge of the door, so he knew that something had happened. So he went and told the rest of them [neighbors]. And they got up a bunch of people and brought them out, one at a time. I believe they said they was fifty men that they brought out, one at a time, before Uncle James. And Uncle James knowed him [Logsdon] as soon as he come around.

Hunter: What were the names of the two sisters who went with Logsdon?

131

Bryant: They was Browns, but I don't know their given names. My daddy stayed all night with one of them, one night, over there the other side of Pleasant Hill. He'd been somewhere back through there and stopped there and stayed all night. And so he said this woman told him about being with them, you know, when they done the killing.[1] And [he] said that she was scared to death, that night, feared that he would get up in the night and kill them [Chuckle].

10. Letter based on oral tradition from Mrs. Ona Barton, Forbus, Tennessee, to Lynwood Montell, April 9, 1979

In talking to my husband's ninety-two-year-old cousin at Byrdstown, she still says her grandmother Margaret Barton, widow of Captain Barton, always said that it was Evans that was connected in the killing. Mrs. Barton was an Evans before her marriage, and she said they were a different set of Evans to her. Now, old Grandma Barton was thirty-one years of age at the time of the murder and lived not much more than a mile from the scene. This cousin seemed to recall perhaps one married a Brown and had one child, but they were separated. I asked about the eight-year-old boy that survived. She, in trying to recall names, mentioned Jimmy.

/s/ Ona

---

1. Jane Brown married James Short after the murders and moved with him to White County, Tennessee, the county where Sam Bryant's father resided. The Shorts were stock traders and often kept people overnight.

The following information about the murders was recorded with pencil and pad.

11. Mrs. Ona Barton, Forbus, Tennessee, November 16, 1977

She knows nothing of the story told by Fred Johnson and company down at the Forbus store about the stunned eight-year-old surviving by falling back into a featherbed and being kept warm for three days. But she did say the little dead boy was found because his hair was sticking out from under the door. She added that the boy was hit with a shovel; the women with an axe.

She mentioned the Evans women supposedly present at the murder, though she didn't want this on tape. Her supposition is that they were prime movers behind the murders, not wanting their father to marry one of the Galloway women. She said that one of the Evans women said to the little boy, after his rescue, "Who hit you?" His answer was, "You ought to know; you were there." There seemed to be no doubt in her mind of the involvement of the Evanses or of the guilt of Logsdon.

12. Mrs. Ona Barton, March 17, 1978

Lish [Elijah] Evans was either the father or brother of the two women who helped Logsdon. They lived on Becky Golman Mountain, now called Koger Mountain. A lot of people feel that Logsdon didn't do the killings; he took the blame on himself.

13. Mrs. Ona Barton, August 7, 1978

Logsdon was courting one of the Evans girls—Fetny or Mandy.

The flood of 1920 in Wolf River Valley was so awesome

that old-timers said of it, "This is just like it was when the Logston Flood came."

14. Mrs. Avo Rains, Byrdstown, Tennessee, January 5, 1978

Had heard her grandfather describe the log saddlebag house the Galloways lived in. Her grandfather was at the hanging. He said that women screamed and cried and fainted when Logsdon was hanged. Logsdon was guilty; everyone felt so, and they still do.

The Galloway women were "seeing men." The Galloway boys were illegitimate. She had passed by the site of the murders with her husband many times. He always discussed the murders when passing by.

The Galloway boy escaped by hiding in a fireplace. She had always heard the rain referred to as occurring on the day of the hanging. Referred to as a "tide."

The Trials

The following are texts of the trial proceedings.

15. Mrs. Flossie Crockett, J. D. Lowrey, Edd Moody, Moodyville, Tennessee, November 16, 1977

Lowrey: He was tried at Jamestown. He was tried at other places, but I don't know where. There was three hearings, from the time he was tried to the time he was hanged. And he was hanged three times. They was three victims. [Laughter] And it was three years from the time he committed the crime to his hanging.

Crockett: They said the little boy identified him; they

would line him up with other men, and then they'd take him [Logsdon] and re-dress him, put different clothes on him, but said the little boy picked him out every time.

Lowrey: And I heard the state's attorney there in Jamestown once said there were three victims, he was tried three times, in three different courts, and it was three years before he was hanged. And he was hanged three times.

Some of them asked him if there was any other party concerned in the murder. And he said it wouldn't help his case any to tell it.

Moody: The Evans sisters must have been the party that helped kill them. They couldn't prove it on them. . . .

Lowrey: They had him in the lineup different times, and the little boy never failed to pick him out. He wanted to kiss the little boy, but the little boy wouldn't come near him, just when they went to hang him.

16. Mrs. C. E. Toney, Allardt, Tennessee, March 3, 1978

Montell: Why did Logsdon take it on himself to protect Jane?

Toney: Well, he didn't have any other choice. You see, there were the three, and there were two witnesses against Cal. And all they [the jury] could do was to take the best evidence in court. Jane and Eliza were actually tried, but they come clear, on account of being the two against Cal; and Cal, they said, didn't make

135

any attempt to try to clear himself when they turned against him.

I'm not sure, but I think Jane was a-courting Cal Logsdon. . . .

That little boy, you know, when they put him on the witness stand, was eight years old.

17. Sam Bryant, Eastland, Tennessee, August 22, 1979

Bryant: Well, they had a bunch of men; I think they had about a hundred men took up. Well, they brought him [Logsdon] around in front of him [Uncle James] and set him down in a chair, you know. And they brought them, one at a time. And they asked him about so-and-so, you know, who he was. . . . So they brought him out when Logston came around. And they asked him, and he . . . jumped up and commenced running backwards. And so they asked him if he knowed the man, and he said "Yeah." Said, "That's him." So that was it. Then they took him out there, and they tried him. . . .

18. Sam Bryant, Eastland, Tennessee, October 17, 1979

Logsdon owned up to it. He owned up to killing them, after they caught him, you know, after they brought him out before Uncle James. And he [the lawman] asked him, before they'd brought him out, says, "Would you know the man, if you was to see him, that done the killing?"

And he said, "Yeah, I'll know him."

And he said, "What does he look like?"

And he said, "He looks just like a devil and nothing else."

So whenever they brought him out, why, they said Uncle James done jumped up and come nigh running backwards, you know, with his hands up. Cause he knew him, just as soon as he seen him.

And all the rest of them in the line-up, he never got up or nothing when they all come by. And so they done had him [Logsdon], you see. And so they got him and arrested him and had court and tried him.

19. Byrd Bryant, Eastland, Tennessee, October 17, 1979

Uncle James was the witness at the trial. This fellow told me, as I said awhile ago, he said they brought three hundred people. And they brought them around one at a time. And he said when they come around to this here fellow, Logston, he [Uncle James] must have been—he was a small boy, at that time. He said they scared him to death; he [Uncle James] broke to run. . . . And they brought these women around. Why, they just scared him to death. [After the tape recorder was turned off, Mr. Bryant recalled that their last name was Brown.]

I've heard Uncle B. Dodson tell this about when he was at the trial, and he told what this fellow had done. The one that used the axe was Logsdon. But they said that he was really scared when they brought him around, when they brought that fellow Logsdon. But he said they hung him.

The Hanging

The following texts are concerned with the hanging.

20. Dennis Crockett, Mrs. Flossie Crockett, J. D. Lowrey, Moodyville, Tennessee, November 16, 1977

Montell: What happened? Why was he hanged three times?

F. Crockett: He broke the rope.

Lowrey: He broke the rope twice at the hanging. There was an old Civil War guerrilla captain there and—do you know what a *withe* is? It's a hickory sprout. You can twist it and beat it and it'll be almost like a rope and stronger than a rope. This old captain said, "Get a withe the next time," after the second time. Some of them said they guessed he had hung people during the war, with withes.

D. Crockett: My grandfather was there.

Lowrey: My grandfather and grandmother was both there. I've heard them tell it.

D. Crockett: Some of them says the first fall broke his neck, but I don't know how they knowed.

F. Crockett: Granny said the hanging was a sight.... They hung him three times; the rope broke.

21. Lonnie Barton, Daily Crouch, Fred Johnson, Forbus, Tennessee, November 16, 1977

Crouch: Logston was hanged in 1872, the year my daddy was born.

Johnson: Uncle Jack Pyle always said that he rode on his casket to the hanging. He set on the box in this two-wheel cart. I've always remembered a song sung there before he was hung:

	"I Ask Not To Live Always." I read about that in Ab Wright's book.
Crouch:	A. B. Wright was the old preacher who preached before he was hanged. Also, Old Man Sam Grear, a former chaplain during the Civil War, was there.
Johnson:	Uncle Jack told me that a lot of people come to the hanging. Said women just fell all over that hill up there.
Barton:	What was that, that they hung him three times? Tried him in three different counties.
Crouch:	Uncle Jack Pyle has told me many times, setting right here on this porch, that two ropes broke that they knotted around. Evidently, they didn't know exactly how. He said Logston kept saying, "Boys, let me go!" Said they strung him up with the third rope, and that time it did the job.
Johnson:	Evidently, they had the ropes too slack, and he fell too far. And he broke it when he fell. Sheriff Taylor is the one who hanged him.

22. Mrs. C. E. Toney, Allardt, Tennessee, March 19, 1978

Sheriff Joe Taylor said, "That man was innocent, or that rope wouldn't have broke. And before I'll hang another man I'll resign my office." He was that sure that he was an innocent man.

She said Cal Logsdon was a clear man. Then, when Uncle Joe Taylor (that was Mr. Ward's, my husband's, uncle) went to hang Cal, and the rope broke, Uncle Joe always said, "That man wasn't guilty, or the rope wouldn't have broke. And it broke twice."

23. Charles Burtram, Cordell Dishman, Mrs. Ona Barton, Lonnie Barton, Sunnybrook, Kentucky, November 10, 1978

Burtram: They built a little old—I guess about an eight-foot-square, boxed-up place, you know, to hang him in, and drove a cart out from under him. And Granddad . . . said when they drove that out from under him, said them men was getting away from there! Granddad seen that he was in there, just his legs just a-swinging, you know. But he was just cutting the awfulest shine, and Granddad said they left there, a lot of men did. They just couldn't stand it.

Dishman: Well, I heard, wasn't he the one the rope broke three times?

Burnett: Didn't Old Man Than Evans, over here on Caney Creek, wasn't he just a boy? Didn't he slip off and go to it? I know he told my father that.

Dishman: Would be about the right age.

L. Barton: He sneaked up through the crowd, got up close to his father. Said his father happened to look and see him. Said his father backhanded him back plumb back through the crowd. Said, "This is no place for a boy."

O. Barton: There was a woman who told me about her grandmother telling that the women made new dresses to go to it. It was a big occasion.

24. Mrs. Sarah Jane Koger, Jamestown, Tennessee, June 18, 1979

Well, Mother and her sister planned to come to the—see the man hung. *Why*, I don't know! But they did. The morning that he was to be hung, why, Mother and her sister backed down and wouldn't come. But I had a uncle that come and seen him hung, and he said the women fainted all over the place. Well, they should have, when they bother to go see something like that.

The following information about the hanging was recorded with pencil and pad.

25. Mrs. Ella Nunn, Albany, Kentucky, unknown date

James P. Gunnels of Pickett County attended Logsdon's hanging. Logsdon was hauled to the place where he was hanged, riding in a wagon pulled by oxen. He was sitting on his black coffin. A group of people were singing, "O Come, Angel Band."

26. Mrs. Mossie Armstrong, Albany, Kentucky, unknown date

Mrs. Armstrong had heard her mother tell the same story as the one related by Mrs. Nunn.

27. Eyewitness description contained in the *Autobiography of the Rev. A. B. Wright*, pp. 96–98.

After filling some appointments in Poplar Cove, I went to Jamestown, where a criminal was in jail, condemned to be hung the next day until he was dead. His name was James Calvin Logston. I had known him when he was a small boy, and had baptized his mother. He was sentenced to hang for killing two women and one child with an ax, the funerals of whom I had preached at their graves. I had been informed that Mr. Logston desired me to preach his funeral, and also wished an early interview with me. On entering the jail, I told him that he had but little more than twenty-four hours to live in this world. I sang a hymn, knelt, and prayed with him. He wept pitifully, and prayed earnestly, but said that he was prepared to die. After giving him some spiritual advice, I left him with the promise to return in a short time. This I did, after taking dinner with the jailer, in company with Brother J. C. Taylor, the sheriff of the county. I advised and prayed with him again.

Late in the day I returned, and found the poor man deeply absorbed in solemn thought, while the sun was pouring in through the grates of the window, for the last time, the closing rays of day. Again I held services with him, and at his request baptized him by pouring, after he had taken upon himself the baptismal covenant. The next morning, taking with me Brother Samuel Grear, I returned to the jail. The poor man told me that he had rested well the night before. After appropriate Scripture reading and song, we all knelt, and Brother Grear led in prayer. In a short time he was shrouded and brought out of jail to a wagon standing at the door. His coffin had been placed in the wagon, which we entered. The driver, Mitchell Wright, and Dr. Graham occupied the seat of the wagon. Dr. J. H. Story and myself occupied the head of the coffin, the criminal the center, and Brothers Grear and Pile the foot. Surrounded by a heavy guard, we moved to the gallows, singing as we went the old hymn, "I would not live alway, I ask not to stay." On arriving at the gallows, the death-warrant from the Supreme Court of the State was read by Mr. S. V. Bowden, a young lawyer of the town. Brother Grear read a Scripture lesson, made a few appropriate remarks, and led in prayer. After this, I preached the funeral of the criminal, from Gen. ix, 6: "Whoso sheddeth man's blood, by man shall his blood be shed." At the close of the sermon the criminal was permitted to shake hands with a large number of his acquaintances. It was a melting scene. He then stated to the crowd that he had come to this end by keeping bad company. At 1:30 P.M. the trigger was sprung; but so soon as he dropped, the rope broke, and he fell suddenly to the ground. Another rope was placed around his neck, and he was drawn up, but had scarcely hung one-half minute when the rope broke a second time, and again he fell to the ground. He then uttered a word or two before they raised him the second time. He hung twenty-five minutes, and was pronounced dead. I remained all this time with him, having promised him that I would do so. His body was cut down, and buried at a short distance west of the town. O, what an awful thing, to see a man in good health so suddenly rushed into eternity!

The Flood Prediction

The texts below deal with the flood:

28. Elvin Byrd, Mrs. Elvin Byrd, Keith Byrd, Albany, Kentucky, February 27, 1976

K. Byrd: What was that you all used to talk about—they hung a man over at Byrdstown that said, "When I die, if I'm innocent it'll rain before . . ."

E. Byrd: That was the Logston Tide. Mama remembers that [story]. It rained three days and nights. There was a Logston man that was supposed to be hung for killing a little girl.

   They hung him, you know. They was a big rain come, you know. It was in Overton County. Here's what he said. He said that he didn't kill no little girl. . . . And he [Logsdon] told them, "To prove that I'm innocent, it's going to rain three days and nights, and tomorrow will be the biggest tide has ever been in Obey River. If I'm innocent, there'll be a three days' and nights' rain. And if it don't rain, I'll be guilty."

And so he told them that he was innocent. And Mama said that Grandpa said that none of them didn't hardly get away from down there till it clouded up and started raining. It rained three days and nights, and they called it the Logston Tide.

29. Keith Byrd, Lucinda Byrd, Albany, Kentucky, March 16, 1976

K. Byrd: And said it would rain three days and three nights.

L. Byrd: Yeah; and it began to rain, and by the time they hung him up.

K. Byrd: Did it really rain three days and nights?

L. Byrd: The rain never ceased!

30. Mrs. Bea Pitman, Albany, Kentucky, March 6, 1976

. . . He told them that the rope would break three times before it killed him, and then he told them it would come the worst flood tide it ever was, and they called it the Logston Tide. It rained for three days and three nights and didn't cease. And they say it was the worst tide that it had been for years.

31. Lonnie Barton, Daily Crouch, Fred Johnson, Forbus, Tennessee, November 16, 1977

Crouch: It came a great rain—a big flood. Old-timers called it "the Cal Logston Tide." Some called it a flood.

Johnson: The Obey River got wild! Called it "the Logston Tide." The rains came on the day he was hanged. My uncle, Jack Pyle, was there the day he was hanged. He was a guard hired to keep people back. He went with the sheriff, Joe Taylor.

32. Mrs. C. E. Toney, Allardt, Tennessee, March 18, 1978

Montell: Ever hear the story about the rain curse?

Toney: Well, it rained, but they wasn't no flood.

33. Charles Burtram, Cordell Dishman, Mrs. Ona Barton, Lonnie Barton, Sunnybrook, Kentucky, November 19, 1978

Montell: I'm interested in the story as you know it about Logsdon and the Logsdon Tide and all of this.

Burtram: I've just got my grandpa's tale, my granddad, we called him. I've heard him tell it different times that they—you was talking about those two big gullies over yonder. They're way-yonder wider than this store. And, of course, they've been timber cut out of it and everything else, you know. They both washed out the day that they hung Logsdon in Jamestown. And he said—now, this is Granddad's tale—he said, "You'll see that you're hanging the wrong man, for they'll come a flood today." And that evening, them gullies washed out. This one up here at Scooger's [one-quarter mile away], you know,

145

Cordell [Dishman]. And then that one from over yonder, you know, on the other side. Granddad said there never was gullies there until that day. And that was called the Logsdon Flood.

Dishman: Yeah, they're up there. The road turns there. You'll go down that road, there is some big gullies. One of them is one of the gullies. Then the other's over west on the far side.

Montell: Had you heard this, too, that they washed out that night?

Dishman: Yes; yes, I've heard that all of my life!

34. Mrs. Sarah Jane Koger, Jamestown, Tennessee, June 18, 1979

But when they hung this man, they come a big flood that night. And Grandmother said that it almost washed everything away where they lived, they was so much water. It was the night he was hung, was what she said.

35. Sam Bryant, Eastland, Tennessee, October 17, 1979

Bryant: Alan told me. He said he heard it that, if he wasn't guilty, there would be a flood; and that if he was guilty, there wouldn't be none. And said that after they hung him—I don't know how long—there come a big flood.

36. Letter based on oral tradition from Mrs. Ona Barton, Forbus, Tennessee, to Lynwood Montell, March 2, 1979

. . . I am finding out more about the flood that I know you will be interested in, but I can't go into details, as some or all of it would be too lengthy. It all bears out that there was a flood. I may be able to find out the name of the family that lived where the rock crusher is. I'm going to make a few telephone calls. . . .

The following information about the flood was recorded with pencil and pad.

37. Mrs. Ona Barton, Forbus, Tennessee, November 16, 1977

She referred to the flood following the hanging as "the Logston Fresh." Says the old-timers called it that before they referred to it as the Tide.

She disavowed any knowledge of the rain story to prove Logsdon's innocence.

38. Mrs. Avo Rains, Byrdstown, Tennessee, September 29, 1980

He told them, to prove he was innocent that it would come the biggest rain ever known. Sure enough, Wolf River had the biggest "tide" ever known, before or since. At an old home-place below Byrdstown—the owner long since dead, I'm told—an old tree still stands where a high-water marker was cut, and it's never reached that far again, by several inches.

Textual Analysis

The following sections present a reconstruction of the events based on a collation of oral traditions with written corroborative evidence. Because this is meant to be just a demonstration and not an exhaustive analysis, only those evidences dealing with the murders themselves and with the flood prediction are dealt with, here. For readers interested in a complete study of this material, it will be published in England as "The Hanging of Calvin Logsdon" in *Folklore Studies in the Twentieth Century*, edited by Venetia Newall.

The Murders

The killer's name was James Calvin Logsdon. Logsdon's identity is never in question. Oral sources seldom refer to him by his first name, calling him simply Logsdon or Logston; trial records identify him as James Calvin Logston. According to a newspaper story, Logsdon maintained that there was no *t* in his name.

His two female accomplices were Jane and Eliza Brown. Oral texts 2 and 9 identify Logsdon's helpers as Jane and Eliza Brown, while texts 3, 5, 7, 10, 12, and 15 claim that their last name was Evans. The contributor of text 7 was emphatic that the women were Evanses and supplied both of their first names. She substantiated her information by claiming that she had known their brother well. The other informants who stated that the women were Evanses based their claims on personal testimonies of parents and grandparents. On the other hand, the contributor of text 2 is the granddaughter of the man who later married Jane Brown and took her to White County. The contributor of text 9 is a resident of White County and is a son of the three-week-old Galloway baby who escaped being murdered. He not only identified the women as Browns, based on family testimony, but he unknowingly corroborated information provided by the contributor of text 2. Text 2 claims that the informant's grandfather was a livestock trader in White County who often kept people overnight. The contributor of text 9 tells that his father spent the night at a house (presumably that mentioned in text 2) whose mistress ironically told of being present when the Galloways were murdered. The evidence afforded by these two texts alone is strong enough to be conclusive that the Brown sisters were indeed involved in the murders.

One deposition taken at Logsdon's hearing identifies his accomplices as Browns, and Jane and Eliza Brown were initially charged in connection with the murders. Another deposition, however, claims that Elisha Evans, brother of Catharine Galloway, paid Logsdon to help him kill the Galloways. Evans, along with his two sons and two daughters, plus Logsdon, went to the Galloway house. "Elisha Evans went to one door and one of the girls went to the other door, and old Mrs. Galloway [his sister] made several attempts to get out and Evans pushed her back three times with a short musket. The others were in the house and killed them [the Galloways]."

After the disagreement in both oral and written sources over identification of the sisters loomed so important, we went into the community and tried to discover the truth. The people we had talked to double-checked among themselves and still agreed conclusively that the guilty women were Evanses, not Browns; nor could any of them remember that the Browns ever lived in the area. Federal Census Schedules were of no assistance in solving the dilemma. Thus, while we are compelled to go along with the name of Brown because of formal murder charges, our knowledge of the tenacity of oral traditions tells us not to push aside lightly the very strong statements in support of the women's being Evanses.

The victims were Galloways and included a mother, her daughter, and the daughter's son. Text 1 states simply that three persons were killed, but does not bother to identify the victims; texts 1, 2, and 5 are correct in claiming the victims included two women and a boy, but still do not mention them by name. Texts 4 and 14 state that there were two women and a boy, and refer to them as Galloways. Texts 6 and 11 refer to them only as Galloways, stating additionally that the victims were a mother, a daughter, and the daughter's son, and that the daughter had two additional children, a boy and a baby girl, who survived.

Internal corroboration is ample to prove that the victims included two Galloway women and a boy, especially with the testimony offered in text 9 by the son of the baby girl who survived, coupled with the fact that only one informant identified the victims by another name. External sources in the form of court records and newspaper accounts, while not really needed for corroboration of the surname, do identify the victims as Catharine, Lucy, and W. B. Galloway, as claimed in text 3.

A small boy and a baby girl survived. Texts 6 and 10 simply state that a little boy managed to survive the slaughter. Text 7 additionally claims that a baby was left unharmed, a claim that is corroborated by texts 8 and 9, whose authors identified the baby who was found on the bed. They also said that the little boy (their uncle) who survived was left on the floor for dead. Texts 4 and 11 claim that a male youngster survived by hiding in a featherbed; text 5, 7, and 14 say he crawled instead to the fireplace, where the warmth of the ashes kept him alive. There is little doubt that the baby girl, being only three weeks old, was left on the bed, while her injured brother crawled on the floor to get closer to the warmth of the fire. Yet, two oral sources substituted the lad for the baby and claimed that it was he who used the featherbed as a means of staying warm.

Only one person who swore a deposition during the lower court proceedings stated that an infant girl survived, although three people testified to a surviving boy. Supreme Court records erroneously state that Lucy Galloway had only two children, making no mention of the infant.

The murders were committed in November 1868. There is no internal agreement among the oral texts as to which night the murders were actually committed. Wednesday, Friday, and Saturday were suggested. Turning to external sources, the Supreme Court proceedings themselves state conflicting nights. At one place November 19 is used, while November 20 is given in another. In his letter to the Supreme Court, Logsdon himself specifies Thursday.

Oral informants agreed that the event occurred during the winter months. Some noted that it was snowing, others simply that it was very cold. The son that survived did so because of warmth provided either by the fireplace ashes (texts 5, 7, and 14) or by a featherbed (texts 4 and 11).

The year 1868 is recorded only in official court records. (Seldom are informants able to give the precise date of an event that happened before their own lifetimes.)

The murdered Galloway family lived in a log house at Possum Trot. Texts 4 and 14 identify the house, but other informants volunteered the same information, although their contributions are not included in the texts printed above. Most, if not all, informants knew the exact site where the old house stood, and one observed that her father told her about the killings every time they passed by the house. This is a good example of how the site of a historical event prompts and stimulates the process of instituting and maintaining a legend.

The three bodies were discovered when a man saw the dead boy's hair sticking under the door. Text 2 claims that the three bodies were discovered by Lucy Galloway's sweetheart, who, seeing the dead boy's hair "sticking out through the crack under the door," reached down to pull the boy's hair, thinking him to be asleep on the floor. Texts 6 and 11 make the same claim in almost identical words, but do not identify the man who spotted the body. Text 7 claims that the visitor was the son of a neighbor, but does not mention the hair episode; and text 9, whose author was the dead boy's nephew, corroborates the hair-pulling scene and identifies the man who found the bodies as a neighbor.

Internal testing results in the logical conclusion that a male neighbor discovered the three bodies. He found them after reaching down to yank in teasing fashion at the little boy's hair. These oral texts alone are enough to persuade us that the boy's hair was indeed seen sticking through the crack under the door, as this scene creates one of the most powerful instances of the use of visual imagery in legend narration that we have encountered. A sworn deposition corroborated these oral testimonies when the speaker observed, "When we found the bodies, W. B. was found lying by the front door."

The Galloway women had bad moral reputations. External sources, such as court proceedings, do not speak to this point, but virtually all oral informants referred to Lucy Galloway with some degree of scorn or social condemnation, and some felt the same way toward Catharine. An examination of the oral texts reveals that Logsdon's female conspirators did not want their father to marry Lucy (texts 2, 5, 11, and 13), thus explaining or corroborating the feelings toward the women's characters expressed by the other informants. The issue of morals appears to have been the basic motive behind the murders. Informants generally felt that, while Logsdon committed the murders, he was persuaded by the sisters to do so. Text 5 claims that the sisters paid Logsdon forty dollars to do the killing. We take such unverifiable statements to be a part of the embellishmental process. They could be true when uttered by someone close to the event, but likely are used by others to lend force and a bit of intrigue to legends.

Logsdon fled the scene of the crime and headed for Kentucky. Texts 1, 4, and 5 all correctly claim that Logsdon was bound for Kentucky, and the last two are both correct in stating that he was detected while crossing the Cumberland River by ferry. Text 4 specifically claims he crossed the Cumberland River by ferry at Burkesville, while text 5 makes an equal claim in favor of the ferry at Rowena. Either could be correct, but most likely he crossed at Rowena, since that place is in direct line with Houstonville, where a sworn deposition indicated Logsdon was apprehended and taken into custody. All sources are silent on the subject of Logsdon's return to Tennessee to stand trial.

The Trials and the Hanging

While texts 15 to 19 contain oral recollections of the three Logsdon trials, their major concern is the manner in which the surviving Galloway boy identified Logsdon as the killer. Oral traditions do not address themselves to the three Supreme Court hearings in Nashville, nor to details surrounding the return of Logsdon to Jamestown for hanging; only the Nashville newspapers did that. Texts 20 to 26 contain oral reminiscences about Logsdon's hanging; text 27 is the account of the hanging described by Rev. A. B. Wright, who personally witnessed the event. Most of the claims about the hanging made in the oral texts are corroborated by the Reverend Mr. Wright's account. Finally, texts 28 to 37 are concerned with the flood predicted by Logsdon on the gallows.

The "Logsdon Tide"

Logically, there are two possibilities regarding the actuality of the flood-producing rain—either it occurred, or it did not. Nothing was written to confirm that it did, and official Weather Bureau records do not reach back to 1872. The only known written eyewitness account of the hanging is contained in the Reverend Mr. Wright's autobiography (text 27), and the flood is not mentioned by him. If, for a moment, we assume that the rain occurred, then the Reverend Mr. Wright may have omitted mention of it for two reasons. First, he did not hear Logsdon's prophecy. This is unlikely, however, since he was with the condemned man during the last hours of his confinement and preached the final sermon at the site of the hanging. Second, the Reverend Mr. Wright refused to mention the prediction because he was a minister, and to most conservative, evangelical mountain preachers then and now, a prophecy of such magnitude as the one pronounced by Logsdon would seem to be the work of Satan.

Oral evidence strongly contends that the rain did occur. First, at least 90 percent of the twenty or more oral infor-

mants verified the rain on the basis of eyewitness testimonies told to them personally by grandparents, other
relatives, and other personal acquaintances who were present at the hanging. Second, the lapse of time between 1872,
when the hanging occurred, and the early childhoods of the
informants was only thirty-five years. If the flood tide was
the product of someone's imagination, the neatly crystallized fabrication is not likely to have so quickly won such
popular acceptance over an eight-county area in two states.
Third, among the persons attesting to the rain were the
widow of the nephew of the sheriff who hanged Logsdon
(text 32), and a son of the baby girl who survived the
Galloway murders (text 35). Fourth, the Logsdon Tide is
identified strongly with particular places and actions
within the Obey-Wolf River valleys where the murders
occurred. It is these affiliations that provide oral informants with emotional ties to history, thus helping them to
recall events from the past. For instance, Charlie Burtram, a
seventy-five-year-old storekeeper in neighboring Wayne
County, Kentucky, pointed to two large present-day gullies
in that community as having been created by the rains
following Logsdon's hanging (text 33).

A resident of the Wolf River Valley, Mrs. Ona Barton,
who is in her late seventies, provided, on August 7, 1978, an
even more vivid illustration of the importance of place and
action to local residents in the crystallization of oral traditional historical narratives as a part of their storytelling
repertoires:

> This old woman lived up here at the foot of Jamestown
> Mountain, where the rock quarry is now, there at the edge of
> Wolf River Valley. She heard this young man—the mail
> carrier—ride up. He was carrying the mail from Jamestown
> down through Wolf River country.

She run out and told him that the valley was flooded, that he would be drowned if he didn't turn around. He said, "But the mail has got to go through," and turned to ride off.
She forcibly pulled him from the horse. It was the awfulest time anybody'd ever seen! Why, that young fellow would have drowned! The Logsdon Tide was all over Wolf River Valley, just a few yards ahead of him. His horse would have gone right into that water and he would have drowned.

Fifth, a proverbial comparison grew out of the Logsdon Tide legend. Cordell Dishman and Charlie Burtram, both lifelong residents of the Chestnut Grove community of Wayne County, Kentucky, located some twenty-five miles from the scene of the hanging, knew of the older local practice of comparing all big rains with the Logsdon-prophesied deluge. Dishman recalled, "I remember when I was growing up and it would come a big rain, they'd say, 'This is almost as big as the Logsdon Flood.' It wasn't as big, though, you see."

The flood itself may not have taken place within the three days prescribed by Logsdon. Eight oral testimonies claimed that the flood occurred, but they are unspecific as to when. One person stated that the flooding came later in the spring. It may be that heavy rains produced flooding a few weeks after the hanging and Logsdon's prediction was recalled at that time. This theory would explain why the rain prophecy did not get into the Reverend Mr. Wright's diary, and further illustrates the process of telescoping (discussed in chapter 2) which, in this instance, provides a fantastic ending to the Logsdon story and an appropriate beginning to the process of legend embellishment—and legend sustenance. Without the rain prophecy and attendant narratives, the Logsdon story likely would have ended at the gallows.

Appendix B

Migratory Legends and Anecdotes

Legends and anecdotes present a knotty problem in local historical research, as they are almost always unverifiable. Furthermore, they are often told in similar form and usually accepted for true in other communities around the country and the world. Historians who have been aware of the floating or migratory nature of many pseudohistorical narratives have often felt frustrated in knowing how to deal with them. Some researchers have incorporated such stories unknowingly into their writings and have been criticized for doing so. In many published local histories, whether the narratives are arranged chronologically or topically, legendary and anecdotal material is often lumped together in a separate chapter, indicating that the author doubted its veracity, but was hesitant to eliminate it altogether, conceding that it had some value, however doubtful that value might be.

Two characteristics distinguish such traditional narratives. First, they are highly localized with regard to names and places, but they are not specific enough to be traced to their origins. When questioned, an informant is likely to say, "I don't know who the person involved was, but my grandmother knew. She's the one who told me about it." Thus, while the events described in these stories *could* have happened, the fact that the same event is reported from some other locality reduces the probability that it ever happened at all. Second, while such stories are plausible enough to lead one to believe they might in fact have happened, they are just "too good to be true." They usually represent people's feelings about possibilities of how things should or might have happened, rather than how they actually occurred.

In our opinion, legends and anecdotes can be valuable complements to written history. These traditional narratives are told within a community about particular places, events, or persons of some significance to residents of the area or members of the group. While the terms *legend* and *anecdote* frequently carry connotations of inaccuracy or outright falsehood, the local historian who wishes to make use of these narrative materials needs to recognize that their significance does not lie in whether they are true or false, but in the fact that they are almost always told and accepted as true.

When the local history researcher is told a narrative that cannot pass the validity tests outlined in chapter 4, and when the story contains one or more rather sensational themes or motifs, the researcher should first check the Thompson indexes, then look into as many regional and topical publications of folk narratives as possible in the quest for parallel occurrences of the narrative in question. Published local histories often contain the only known reports of these narratives, so do not overlook these very likely sources. The following summaries of migratory narratives include only some of the more common ones. Once one establishes a sensitivity to or a "feel" for these kinds of stories, it becomes easier to identify probable instances readily.

The Dream Contest

An Indian chief tells a white man of a dream in which the white man gave the Indian his red coat. Then the white man "dreams" that the Indian gave him vast tracts of land, and the Indian is forced to do so, commenting that he will never dream with the white man again.

Panther on the Roof

A frontier woman alone (or with small children) in the house keeps a panther at bay by tossing it bones and other items of food, or by maintaining a roaring fire in the fireplace, until help comes.

Panther in Pursuit

A frontier heroine, caught away from the house, is able to elude a pursuing panther by removing articles of her clothing and tossing them into the path of the oncoming animal, which stops to sniff each item, until she reaches safety.

The Death Car

A new automobile is on sale at a local dealer's at a real "steal," the reason being the ineradicable stench of death that has clung to the vehicle ever since a decomposed human body was found in it.

The Fork in the Skirt

A young woman, who boasts to her friends of being unafraid of ghosts, is found dead (or in a faint) slumped over a grave. A kitchen fork (or knife) has her skirt pinned to the ground. (This is Tale Type 1676(b).)

The Numbskull Apprentice

A physician tells a patient that he is sick from eating too many boiled eggs, then explains to his young apprentice that he had seen egg shells under the man's bed. The apprentice goes alone to visit a patient; he diagnoses the patient's problem as overconsumption of horse meat. He had spotted a saddle under the bed. (This is a variant of Tale Type 1862C.)

Person Saved from Live Burial

Eyelash flickers as person is about to be lowered into the grave.

Doomed Man Rides on Coffin and Plays Fiddle on Way to the Gallows

Man offers his fiddle to anyone who can outplay him. Following the execution, the hanged man's body is removed from coffin; coffin is buried empty, while the body is cared for in some special way. Years later, another person confesses to the murder for which the man was hanged.

Bibliography of Works Cited

BOOKS AND DISSERTATIONS

Allen, Barbara. "Talking about the Past: A Folkloristic Study of Orally Communicated History." Ph.D. dissertation, University of California at Los Angeles, 1980.

Alvarez, Ronald A. F., and Susan C. Kline. *Self-Discovery through the Humanities, I: Exploring Local History.* Washington: The National Council on the Aging, Inc., 1977.

Baughman, Ernest W. *Type and Motif-Index of the Folktales of England and North America.* Bloomington: Indiana University Press, 1966.

Baum, Willa K. *Oral History for the Local Historical Society.* Second edition, revised. Nashville: American Association for State and Local History, 1971.

Bloch, Marc. *French Rural History: An Essay on Its Basic Characteristics.* Translated by Janet Sondheimer. Berkeley: University of California Press, 1970.

Chambers, E. K. *Arthur of Britain.* London: Sidgwick and Jackson, Ltd., 1927.

Christiansen, Reidar Th. "The Migratory Legends." Folklore Fellows Communication, No. 175. Helsinki: Suomalainen Tiedeakatemia, 1958.

161

Clarke, Kenneth W. *Uncle Bud Long: The Birth of a Kentucky Folk Legend.* Lexington: The University Press of Kentucky, 1973.

Couch, William, ed. *These Are Our Lives.* Chapel Hill: University of North Carolina Press, 1939.

Davis, Cullom, Kathryn Back, and Kay MacLean. *Oral History: From Tape to Type.* Chicago: American Library Association, 1977.

DeCaro, Francis A. "Folklore as an 'Historical Science': The Anglo-American Viewpoint." Ph.D. dissertation, Indiana University, 1973.

DeCell, Harriet C., and JoAnne Prichard. *Yazoo: Its Legends and Legacies.* Yazoo City: Yazoo Delta Press, 1976.

Dobie, J. Frank. *Legends of Texas.* Publications of the Texas Folklore Society, No. 3. Dallas: Southern Methodist University Press, 1924.

Dorson, Richard M. *American Folklore and the Historian.* Chicago: University of Chicago Press, 1971.

————. *Bloodstoppers and Bearwalkers: Folk Traditions from Michigan's Upper Peninsula.* Cambridge: Harvard University Press, 1952.

————. *Jonathan Draws the Long Bow: New England Popular Tales and Legends.* Cambridge: Harvard University Press, 1946.

Evans, George Ewart. *The Days That We Have Seen.* London: Faber and Faber, 1975.

Febvre, Lucian. *A New Kind of History: From the Writings of Lucian Febvre.* Edited by Peter Burke. Translated by F. Folca. New York: Harper and Row, 1973.

Fife, Austin, and Alta Fife. *Saints of Sage and Saddle: Folklore among the Mormons.* Bloomington: Indiana University Press, 1956.

Fry, Gladys-Marie. *Night Riders in Black Folk History.* Knoxville: University of Tennessee Press, 1975.

Furay, Conal. *The Grass-Roots Mind in America: The American Sense of Absolutes.* New York: New Viewpoints, 1977.

Gallagher, Dorothy. *Hannah's Daughters: Six Generations of an American Family, 1876–1976.* New York: Thomas Y. Crowell, 1976.

Goldstein, Kenneth S. *A Guide for Field Workers in Folklore.* Hatboro, Pa.: Folklore Associates, 1964.

Granger, Byrd Howell. *A Motif Index for Lost Mines and Treasures.* Tucson: University of Arizona Press, 1977.

Greven, Philip J. *Four Generations: Population, Land, and Family in Colonial America.* Ithaca: Cornell University Press, 1970.

Hockett, Homer C. *The Critical Method in Historical Research and Writing.* Third edition. New York: Macmillan, 1955.

Holmes, Urban Tigner, Jr. *Daily Living in the Twelfth Century.* Madison: University of Wisconsin Press, 1962.

Ives, Edward D. *The Tape-Recorded Interview: A Manual for Field Workers in Folklore and Oral History.* Knoxville: University of Tennessee Press, 1980.

Joyner, Charles W. *Slave Folklife: Antebellum Black Culture in the South Carolina Low Country.* Urbana: University of Illinois Press, forthcoming.

Kirshenblatt-Gimblett, Barbara. "Traditional Storytelling in the Toronto Jewish Community: A Study in Performance and Creativity in an Immigrant Culture." Ph.D. dissertation, Indiana University, 1972.

Liestøl, Knut. *The Origin of the Icelandic Family Sagas.* Oslo: H. Aschehoug and Co., 1930.

Long, Reuben A., and E. R. Jackman. *The Oregon Desert.* Caldwell, Ida.: Caxton Printers, 1964.

MLA Handbook for Writers of Research Papers, Theses, and Dissertations. New York: Modern Language Association, 1977.

Martin, Charles. "Hollybush: The Eclipse of the Traditional Building System in a Mountain Community: An Architectural and Oral Historical Study." Ph.D. dissertation, Indiana University, 1980.

McCall, Daniel F. *Africa in Time Perspective: A Discussion of Historical Reconstruction from Unwritten Sources.* London: Oxford University Press, 1969.

Mitchell, Roger E. *I'm a Man That Works: The Biography of Don Mitchell of Merrill, Maine.* Orono, Me.: Northeast Folklore Society, 1978.

Montell, William Lynwood. *The Saga of Coe Ridge: A Study in Oral History.* Knoxville: University of Tennessee Press, 1970.

Moss, William W. *Oral History Program Manual.* New York: Praeger, 1974.

Neely, Charles. *Tales and Songs of Southern Illinois.* Menasha, Wisc.: George Banta Publishing Co., 1938.

Picken, Andrew. *Traditionary Stories of Old Families, and Legendary Illustrations of Family History.* Two vols. London: Long and Long, 1833.

Rosengarten, Theodore [and Nate Shaw]. *All God's Dangers: The Life of Nate Shaw.* New York: Alfred A. Knopf, 1974.

Russo, David. *Families and Communities: A New View of American History.* Nashville: American Association for State and Local History, 1974.

Shumway, Gary L., and William G. Hartley. *An Oral History Primer.* Fullerton, Calif.: California State University at Fullerton, 1973.

Smith, Page. *A New Age Now Begins: A People's History of the American Revolution.* Two vols. New York: McGraw-Hill, 1976.

Stahl, Sandra K. D. "The Personal Narrative as a Folklore Genre." Ph.D. dissertation, Indiana University, 1975.

Stoffle, Richard W., and Michael J. Evans. *Kaibab Paiute History: The Early Years.* Fredonia, Ariz.: Kaibab Paiute Council, 1978.

Terrill, Tom, and Jerrold Hirsch, eds. *Such As Us: Southern Voices of the Thirties.* Chapel Hill: University of North Carolina Press, 1978.

Thernstrom, Stephan. *Poverty and Progress: Social Mobility in a Nineteenth-Century City.* Cambridge: Harvard University Press, 1964.

Thompson, Edward P. *The Making of the English Working Class.* New York: Pantheon Books, 1964.

Thompson, Paul. *The Voice of the Past: Oral History.* Oxford: Oxford University Press, 1978.

Thompson, Stith. *Motif-Index of Folk Literature.* Six vols. Bloomington: Indiana University Press, 1955–1958.

———. *The Types of the Folktale.* Revised edition. Helsinki: Suomalainen Tiedeakatemia, 1961.

Turabian, Kate. *A Manual for Writers of Term Papers, Theses, and Dissertations.* Fourth ed. Chicago: University of Chicago Press, 1973.

Vansina, Jan. *Oral Tradition: A Study in Historical Methodology.* Translated by H. M. Wright. Chicago: Aldine Publishing Co., 1965.

White, Rev. C. C., and Ada M. Holland. *No Quittin' Sense.* Austin: University of Texas Press, 1969.

Woods, Barbara Allen. *The Devil in Dog Form: A Partial Type-Index of Devil Legends.* Berkeley: University of California Folklore Studies, No. 11, 1959.

Wright, Rev. J. D., ed. *Autobiography of Rev. A. B. Wright of the Holston Conference, M.E. Church.* Cincinnati: Cranston and Curts, 1896. Reprint. Jamestown, Tenn.: Fentress County Historical Society, 1978.

JOURNAL ARTICLES

Aceves, Peter R. "The Hillsville Tragedy in Court Record, Mass Media, and Folk Balladry." *Keystone Folklore Quarterly* 16 (1971): 1–38.

Allen, Barbara. "Personal Experience Narratives: Use and Meaning in Interaction." *Folklore and Mythology Studies* 2 (1978): 5–7.

———. "The Personal Point of View in Orally Communicated History." *Western Folklore* 38 (1979): 110–118.

Bassett, T. D. Seymour. "The Cold Summer of 1816 in Vermont." *New England Galaxy* 15 (1973): 15–19.

Davidson, H. R. Ellis. "Folklore and History." *Folklore* 85 (1974): 73–92.

Dorson, Richard M. "Sources for the Traditional History of the Scottish Highlands and Western Islands." *Journal of the Folklore Institute* 8 (1971): 147–184.

Dupree, Louis. "The Retreat of the British Army from Kabul to Jalalabad in 1842: Folklore and History." *Journal of the Folklore Institute* 4 (1967): 50–74.

Hudson, Charles. "Folk History and Ethnohistory." *Ethnohistory* 13 (1966): 52–70.

Hurst, Richard. "History and Folklore." *New York Folklore Quarterly* 25 (1969): 243–260.

Ivey, William. " 'The 1913 Disaster': Michigan Local Legend." *Folklore Forum* 3 (1970): 100–114.

Kalčik, Susan. "Like Ann's Gynecologist . . . : Personal Narratives in Women's Rap Groups." *Journal of American Folklore* 88 (1975): 3–11.

McDonald, Donald. "A Visual Memory." *Scottish Studies* 22 (1978): 1–26.

Mitchell, Carol A. "The White House." *Indiana Folklore* 2 (1969): 97–109.

Nicolaisen, W. F. H. "Some Humorous Folk-Etymological Narratives." *New York Folklore Quarterly* 3 (1977): 1–13.

Seager, Robert II. "American Folklore and History: Observations on Potential Integration." *Midwest Folklore* 1 (1951): 213–222.

Wilder, Amos N. "Between Reminiscence and History." *Massachusetts Historical Society Proceedings* 87 (1975): 105–117.

Wylie, Kenneth C. "The Uses and Misuses of Ethnohistory." *Journal of Interdisciplinary History* 3 (1973): 707–720.

ARTICLES IN BOOKS

Boatright, Mody C. "The Family Saga as a Form of Folklore." In *The Family Saga and Other Phases of American Folklore,* edited by Mody C. Boatright, pp. 1–19. Urbana: University of Illinois Press, 1958.

Dorson, Richard M. "The Debate over the Trustworthiness of Oral Traditional History." Reprinted in *Folklore: Selected Essays*, pp. 199–223. Bloomington: Indiana University Press, 1972.

———. "The Oral Historian and the Folklorist." In *Selections from the Fifth and Sixth National Colloquia on Oral History*, edited by Peter D. Olch and Forrest C. Pogue, pp. 40–49. New York: Oral History Association, 1972.

Glassie, Henry. "A Folkloristic Thought on the Promise of Oral History." In *Selections from the Fifth and Sixth National Colloquia on Oral History*, edited by Peter D. Olch and Forrest C. Pogue, pp. 54–57. New York: Oral History Association, 1972.

Halpert, Herbert. " 'Egypt'—A Wandering Place-Name Legend." In *Buying the Wind: Regional Folklore in the United States*, by Richard M. Dorson, pp. 295–299. Chicago: University of Chicago Press, 1964.

Ives, Edward D. "Common Man Biography." In *Folklore Today: A Festschrift for Richard M. Dorson*, edited by Linda Dégh, Henry Glassie, and Felix Oinas, pp. 251–264. Bloomington: Indiana University Press, 1976.

Wilgus, D. K., and Lynwood Montell. "Beanie Short: A Civil War Chronicle in Legend and Song." In *American Folk Legend: A Symposium*, edited by Wayland D. Hand, pp. 133–156. Berkeley: University of California Press, 1971.

MANUSCRIPTS

Conard, Rebecca. "The Family Farm: A Study of Folklife in Historical Context." Paper delivered to the American Folklore Society, October 1979, at Los Angeles, Calif.

MacGregor-Villarreal, Mary. "Team Research: Are Two Heads Necessarily Better Than One?" Paper delivered to the California Folklore Society, April 1979, at Los Angeles, Cal.

Martin, Charles. Letter to Lynwood Montell, March 27, 1980.

BIBLIOGRAPHY

NEWSPAPERS

"Buick Says Bradley Rode to Get Dr. Daly in 1894." *Lake County Examiner*, November 27, 1969, p. 3.

ORAL SOURCES

Armstrong, Mossie. Tape-recorded interview. Albany, Kentucky, 1977.

Barton, Lonnie. Tape-recorded interview. Forbus, Tennessee, November 16, 1977; Chestnut Grove, Kentucky, November 10, 1978.

Barton, Ona. Tape-recorded interview. Chestnut Grove, Kentucky, November 10, 1978; Jamestown, Tennessee, June 18, 1979.

Barton, Ona. Recorded with pencil and pad. Forbus, Tennessee, November 16, 1977; March 17, 1978; and August 7, 1978.

Barton, Ona. Letters. Forbus, Tennessee, January 10, 1978; April 9, 1979.

Boatwright, Genevieve. Tape-recorded interview. Fort Rock, Oregon, July 4, 1978.

Bryant, Byrd. Tape-recorded interview. Eastland, Tennessee, October 17, 1979.

Bryant, Rosie. Tape-recorded interview. Whitley City, Kentucky, May 8, 1979. Lake Cumberland Library District Oral History Project, Burkesville, Kentucky.

Bryant, Sam. Tape-recorded interview. Eastland, Tennessee, August 22, 1979; and October 17, 1979.

Burnett, Sherman. Tape-recorded interview. Chestnut Grove, Kentucky, November 10, 1978.

Burtram, Charles. Tape-recorded interview. Chestnut Grove, Kentucky, November 10, 1978; and November 19, 1978.

Byrd, Elvin. Tape-recorded interview. Albany, Kentucky, February 27, 1976.

Byrd, Mrs. Elvin. Tape-recorded interview. Albany, Kentucky, February 27, 1976.

Byrd, Keith. Tape-recorded interview. Albany, Kentucky, February 27, 1976, and March 16, 1976.

Byrd, Lucinda. Tape-recorded interview. Albany, Kentucky, March 16, 1976.

Coe, Escar O. Tape-recorded interview. Burkesville, Kentucky, October 17, 1975.

Coe, Tim. Informal conversation. Burkesville, Kentucky, June 2, 1961.

Copeland, Coyle. Tape-recorded interview. Crawford, Tennessee, May 15, 1976.

Crockett, Dennis. Tape-recorded interview. Moodyville, Tennessee, November 16, 1977.

Crockett, Flossie. Tape-recorded interview. Moodyville, Tennessee, November 16, 1977.

Crouch, Daily. Tape-recorded interview. Forbus, Tennessee, November 16, 1977.

Dishman, Cordell. Tape-recorded interview. Chestnut Grove, Kentucky, November 10, 1978, and November 19, 1978.

Emery, Russell and Mary. Tape-recorded interview. Silver Lake, Oregon, August 8, 1978.

Eskelin, Edwin. Tape-recorded interview. Fort Rock, Oregon, July 12, 1978.

Ettinger, Edwin. Tape-recorded interview. San Clemente, California, July 4, 1977.

Iverson, Marge. Tape-recorded interview. Silver Lake, Oregon, July 6, 1978.

Johnson, Fred. Tape-recorded interview. Forbus, Tennessee, November 16, 1977.

Koger, Sarah Jane. Tape-recorded interview. Jamestown, Tennessee, June 18, 1979.

Lowe, Mary Lucy. Tape-recorded interview. Columbia, Kentucky, December 5, 1978. Lake Cumberland Library District Oral History Project, Burkesville, Kentucky.

Lowrey, J. D. Tape-recorded interview. Moodyville, Tennessee, November 16, 1977.

Montell, Willie. Recorded with pencil and pad. Rock Bridge, Monroe County, Kentucky, November 26, 1977.

Moody, Edd. Tape-recorded interview. Moodyville, Tennessee, November 16, 1977.

BIBLIOGRAPHY

Morrison, Sidney. Tape-recorded interview. Bear River Valley, California, July 26, 1974.
Nunn, Ella. Tape-recorded interview. Albany, Kentucky, 1977.
Patton, George. Tape-recorded interview. Forbus, Tennessee, February 12, 1972.
Pittman, Lilly Bea Byrd. Tape-recorded interview. Albany, Kentucky, March 6, 1976.
Rains, Avo. Recorded with pencil and pad. Byrdstown, Tennessee, January 5, 1978, and September 29, 1980.
Standridge, Willie. Archive of Folklore, Folklife, and Oral History, Western Kentucky University, Bowling Green, Kentucky. Unaccessioned tape.
Stratton, Forest. Tape-recorded interview. Silver Lake, Oregon, July 8, 1978.
Toney, Mrs. C. E. Tape-recorded interview. Allardt, Tennessee, March 3, 18, 19, 1978.
Tooley, Sarah. Tape-recorded interview. Fountain Run, Kentucky, August 20, 1961.
Warner, Neva. Tape-recorded interview. Silver Lake, Oregon, July 6, 1978.
Wood, Norman, and Mae Wood. Tape-recorded interview. Jamestown, Tennessee, June 18, 1979.

Index

Accuracy: of orally communicated history. *See* Validity, of orally communicated history
Anecdotes, 52–53, 73, 105

Ballads and songs, 89, 90, 92–93
Bias: of informants, 82–83; of researchers, 93, 109, 111–112

Chronology: in orally communicated history, 26–29
Community history: narrative clustering in, 31–33; as topic of orally communicated history, 50–52; key events in, 98–100
Community identity, 42, 97–98
Corroboration: of orally communicated history: 37–38, 84–87, 110. *See also* Orally communicated history
Customs, 17, 62–63, 75–76

Dating events by association, 26–27, 60, 81, 110
Displacement of characters: in orally communicated history, 36–38

Embellishment, 39, 74–76, 78–79

Emotion: in orally communicated history, 29–31, 91–92
Ethnohistory, 8–9

Family history, 39–40, 48–49, 69–70, 96–97
Fictitious names, use of, 111
Folk etymology, 50
Folk history, 9–11
Folklore, 23–24, 71–74, 105

Genealogy, 36, 69–70

Heroes, 52–53, 94, 95
Historico-motifs, 38–39, 72–73

Informants, 10, 81–83
Interviewing, 43–44, 102–103

Kernel narratives, 44–45

Legal release and responsibility, 10, 102–103, 111
Legends, historical, 73, 84, 97, 105
Life histories, 63–64
Local historian, 3–4

171

Local history: and attitudes of academic historians, 4–5; definition, 4–5; as microcosm of national and regional history, 5–6; sensitive subjects in, 12–13, 57, 111; events in, as topics of orally communicated history, 51–52; key events in, 98–100

Local history research: possible topics of, 7, 44–45; use of orally communicated history in, 14–22, 54–65

Local landmarks, 50–51

Manuscript preparation, 101–114

Material culture, 15–17, 64, 75–76, 83–84

"Megastory," 32–33

Memory: secondary materials derived from, 22, 60–61; mentioned, 16, 20, 68

Migration of dramatic narrative elements. See Motif

Migratory narratives, 52, 73–74, 79–80

Motif, 26, 38–39, 71–73, 78, 95

Narrative clustering, 31–33

Occupations: as topics of orally communicated history, 49–50

Oral history, 23–24

Orally communicated history: as complement to written records, 3, 18–19, 58–60, 104–105; reconstructing the past with, 8–11, 64, 67–68; use in local history research, 14–22, 51, 54–65; and material culture, 15–17, 64, 75–76, 83–84; as supplement to written records, 15–17, 43, 54–57; validity of, 16, 67–100, 115–156; everyday aspects of the past in, 17, 60–64; contrasted with formal history, 18, 21–23, 25, 58–61, 98–99; personal view of history in, 18–22, 27, 82; as primary source of information about the past, 19–20, 60–65, 67–68, 104; characteristics of, 20–22, 25–40, 86, 100; attitudes,

values, and beliefs expressed in, 21–22, 33, 44, 82–83, 89–100; chronological configuration of, 22, 28–29; mental associations in, 29–31, 44; patterning in, 39–40, 49; social settings for, 40–45; varying points of view in, 52, 76–79, 92–95, 109–110; human element of history in, 56–60, 91–92, 102, 107; logical nature of, 79–80; submerged truths in, 89–100; mentioned, 68. See also Chronology; Corroboration; Displacement of characters; Emotion; Occupations; Patterning; Validity; Visual imagery

Outlaws, 40, 52–53, 94–95

Patterning: in orally communicated history, 39–40, 49

Personal-experience narratives: as patterned forms of expression, 39; as topics of orally communicated history, 47–48, 60; as eyewitness accounts, 55, 58–59, 106

Place names, 50–51, 97, 105

Proverbs, 89, 91

Reminiscence, 41–43

Researcher: as community insider, 11–13; as outsider, 11, 13–14; sex and ethnic background of, 13–14

"Sagamen," 48

Social history, 5, 61n

Symbols, 34–35

Telescoping: of historical time, 35–36

Transcribing tapes, 10, 103

Validity, of orally communicated history: internal tests for, 32, 71–83; external tests for, 32, 83–87; argument for, 67–71; in submerged form, 89–100, 105; case study of, 115–156

Villains, 52–53

Visual imagery: in orally communicated history, 33–35, 39, 79

172

HIGHSMITH 45-102

PRINTED IN U.S.A.